MATH PHONICS™

MULTIPLICATION

Quick Tips and Alternative Techniques for Math Mastery

BY MARILYN B. HEIN
ILLUSTRATED BY RON WHEELER

Teaching & Learning Company

1204 Buchanan St., P.O. Box 10
Carthage, IL 62321

THIS BOOK BELONGS TO

Cover by Ron Wheeler

Copyright © 1996, Teaching & Learning Company

ISBN No. 1-57310-069-2

Printing No. 9876

Teaching & Learning Company
1204 Buchanan St., P.O. Box 10
Carthage, IL 62321

Math Phonics™ is a trademark registered to Marilyn B. Hein.

TABLE OF CONTENTS

NOTE TO PARENTS

Although this book has been specifically designed to be used by classroom teachers for teaching multiplication facts, the materials are extremely helpful when used by parents and children at home.

If you have purchased this book to use at home with your child, I recommend that all of the fill-in-the-blank pages be inserted into vinyl page protectors and worked with a dry-erase overhead transparency marker. The page protectors can be washed and the page can be reused. Put all the page protectors and worksheets into a vinyl, two-pocket binder. The pen, flash cards and other materials can be kept in the binder pockets, thus creating a handy, portable math kit.

I think you will find that these methods work extremely well both at home and in the classroom. It's a book you can count on!

ACKNOWLEDGEMENTS

A special thanks to all these people who have helped and supported me in my work on *Math Phonics™—Multiplication*: Lorraine Jeter who was the first to listen and give me her vote of confidence; Diane Degood who taught me word processing in her "spare" time; Principal Larry Conrardy who allowed me to offer my materials to his teachers at St. Francis School in Wichita, Kansas; Mary Lou Harding for helping me film a demonstration video; Sandi Rongish for her time and support; Bonnie Sheahon, Kay Suchan, Becky Low, Julie Stuckey, Diana Dechant, Melissa Peterson and Cindy Goodwin for listening and trying some of my suggestions; and to Walter Lohrentz, who taught me to multiply. A special thanks to Wesley Learned and Judy Mitchell for their detailed suggestions which helped me to finally devise the best format. Lastly, thanks to God the father for giving me the gift of life.

DEDICATION

To my husband, Joe, who has always supported me through my many and varied projects.
To my children who always motivate me.

Dear Teacher or Parent,

I have always loved math! My mother taught grade school math for 31 years, and she was constantly showing me shortcuts, tricks, math puzzles and games. I thought math was fun (except for long division!). I earned a bachelor of science degree in mathematics in 1968, and in the years since I have taught junior high school math; tutored in my home; worked as a substitute teacher for K-8; worked as a classroom aide in second, third and fourth grades and raised our six children.

When one of my children announced to me in second grade that she "hated math," I knew I had to do something to help her. I started to recall all the methods that were used during my grade school years that I no longer saw being used in classrooms today. I started remembering all the memory "tricks" I had made up to help me memorize the multiplication facts. I organized them in my mind and started teaching them to my daughter. She had nearly mastered multiplication before they started it at school. When they did start, the change was very obvious to me. Instead of the "F" math papers she had frequently brought home in the past, the papers began to be "Bs" and "As."

Several weeks later, my daughter brought home an assignment in which she was to name her favorite subject. She had written *math*. I asked her if she realized what she had written. She replied, "Oh, math is fun because it's easy."

I have now organized my ideas into this classroom enrichment program which I have entitled *Math Phonics™*. I hope you enjoy working with these materials as much as I have!

Sincerely,

Marilyn

Marilyn B. Hein

TLC10069 Copyright © Teaching & Learning Company, Carthage, IL 62321

WHAT IS MATH PHONICS™?

Math Phonics™ is a specially designed program for teaching multiplication facts initially or for remedial work.

WHY IS IT CALLED MATH PHONICS™?

In reading, phonics is used to group similar words, and it teaches the students simple rules for pronouncing each word.

In *Math Phonics*™, math facts are grouped and learned by means of simple patterns, rules and mnemonic devices.

In reading, phonics develops mastery by repetitive use of words already learned.

Math Phonics™ uses drill and review to reinforce students' understanding.

HOW WAS MATH PHONICS™ DEVELOPED?

Why did "Johnny" have so much trouble learning to read during the years that phonics was dropped from the curriculum of many schools in this country? For the most part, he had to simply memorize every single word in order to learn to read, an overwhelming task for a young child. If he had an excellent memory or a knack for noticing patterns in words, he had an easier time of it. If he lacked those skills, learning to read was a nightmare, often ending in failure–failure to learn to read and failure in school.

Phonics seems to help many children learn to read more easily. Why? When a young child learns one phonics rule, that one rule unlocks the pronunciation of dozens or even hundreds of words. It also provides the key to parts of many larger words. The trend in U.S. schools today seems to be to include phonics in the curriculum because of the value of that particular system of learning.

As a substitute teacher, I have noticed that math teacher manuals sometimes have some valuable phonics-like memory tools for teachers to share with students to help them memorize math facts–the addition, subtraction, multiplication and division facts which are the building blocks of arithmetic. However, much of what I remembered from my own education was not contained in the available materials. I decided to create my own materials based upon what I had learned during the past 40 years as a student, teacher and parent.

The name *Math Phonics*™ occurred to me because the rules, patterns and memory techniques that I have assembled are similar to language arts phonics in several ways. Most of these rules are short and easy to learn. Children are taught to look for patterns and use them as "crutches" for coming up with the answer quickly. Some groups have similarities so that learning one group makes it easier to learn another. Last of all, *Math Phonics*™ relies on lots of drill and review, just as language arts phonics does.

Children *must* master addition, subtraction, multiplication and division facts and the sooner the better. When I taught seventh and eighth grade math over 20 years ago, I was amazed at the number of students who had not mastered the basic math facts. At the that time, I had no idea how to help them. My college math classes did not give me any preparation for that situation. I had not yet delved into my personal memory bank to try to remember how I had mastered those facts.

When my six children had problems in that area, I was strongly motivated to give some serious thought to the topic. I knew my children had to master math facts, and I needed to come up with additional ways to help them. For kids to progress past the lower grades without a thorough knowledge of those facts would be like trying to learn to read without knowing the alphabet.

I have always marveled at the large number of people who tell me that they "hated math" when they were kids. I wonder how many of them struggled with the basic math facts when they needed to have them clearly in mind. I firmly believe that a widespread use of *Math Phonics*™ could be a tremendous help in solving the problem of "math phobia."

WHAT ARE THE PRINCIPLES OF MATH PHONICS™?

There are three underlying principles of *Math Phonics*™.
They are: 1. Understanding
2. Learning
3. Mastery
Here is a brief explanation of the meaning of these principles.

1. **UNDERSTANDING:** All true mathematical concepts are abstract which means they can't be touched. They exist in the mind. For most of us, understanding such concepts is much easier if they can be related to something in the real world–something that can be touched.

Thus I encourage teachers and parents to find concrete examples of multiplication facts. For example, a carton of eggs is an excellent example of 2 x 6 = 12. For 3 x 4 = 12, three rows of objects with four objects in each row can be arranged to demonstrate that fact.

Next we use the base 10 counting chart as a shortcut to the same answer. If a child has seen the multiplication facts demonstrated by use of objects or the counting chart, she is much more likely to learn and master them.

2. **LEARNING:** Here is where the rules and patterns mentioned earlier play an important part. A child can be taught a simple rule and on the basis of that, call to mind a whole set of math facts. But the learning necessary for the addition, subtraction, multiplication and division facts must be firmly in place so that the information will be remembered next week, next month and several years from now. That brings us to the next principle.

3. **MASTERY:** We have all had the experience of memorizing some information for a test or quiz tomorrow and then promptly forgetting most of it. This type of memorization will not work for the math facts. In order for children to master these facts, *Math Phonics*™ provides visual illustrations, wall charts, flash cards, practice sheets, worksheets and games. Some children may only need one or two of these materials, but there are plenty from which to choose for those who need more.

You will want to purchase or create a pocket folder for each student to keep all the *Math Phonics*™ materials at home.

Inexpensive pocket folders are available at many school or office supply stores, discount stores or other outlets.

An easy-to-make pocket folder can be made from a large paper grocery or shopping bag.

1. Cut away the bottom of the bag and discard.

2. Cut open along one long side and lay flat.

3. Pick one of the folds and measure out 10" (25 cm) from the fold on either side. Trim bag.

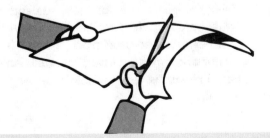

4. Now measure 12" (30 cm) down from the top and fold up the remaining portion of the bag.

5. Staple pockets at outside edges and fold in half.

6. Decorate front and back.

Suggest to parents that children should keep all of their *Math Phonics*™ materials (worksheets, travel folders, progress charts, etc.) in this folder. Parents may also wish to supply clear plastic page protectors and dry-erase markers. Worksheets can be inserted into the page protectors, completed with the dry-erase marker and reused. (See note on page 12.)

SUMMARY OF THE 10 BASIC STEPS

1. Teach the Concept of Multiplication

Multiplication is the shortcut to adding the same number several times. Many third graders know what the term means and understand the concept, but some do not. Materials are included in this Math Phonics™ program to clearly demonstrate and explain this concept.

2. Teach the Perfect Squares

The Perfect Squares are the multiplication facts in which both of the numbers being multiplied are the same. These have a certain artistic appeal to many people. This is a very important group of multiplication facts because in algebra, it is important to have a good memory for squares and square roots in order to solve the final term in a quadratic equation. Also, I believe that these are easier to learn if they are taken as a group and learned first because the answers are spaced fairly far apart on the number line—there's one answer in the teens, $4 \times 4 = 16$; one in the twenties, $5 \times 5 = 25$ and so on. It's easier to learn these if they are taught before all the other answers near them are studied.

3. Teach the 9s

Many people think the 9s are hard to learn, but when students are shown the patterns and how to make use of them, they find that 9s are really rather easy.

4. Teach the 0s, 1s and 2s

After those two challenging groups, we will jump to two groups which most students find much easier. It might seem unnecessary to work on these two groups, but as simple as they seem, some students get confused because adding zero and multiplying by zero do not give the same answer, just as adding one and multiplying by one do not give the same answer.

5. Teach the 2s

Again, this group should be fairly easy for most students, especially if they have mastered the doubles in addition. The doubles in addition are those problems in which both numbers being added are the same. That is, if students know that $5 + 5 = 10$, you can demonstrate that this gives the same answer as $5 \times 2 = 10$.

6. Teach 10s, 11s and 12s

Teaching 10s and 11s should be easy once students understand the memory tools which will be discussed in the next section. The 12s group will be related to the 11s group and should then be fairly simple to teach.

7. Teach the 5s

Most students have learned to count by 5s in second grade because of telling time and counting money. This ability will be used in order to teach the 5s multiplication facts.

8. Teach the 3s and 4s

Threes and 4s are tricky for students to learn because the answers are closely spaced. If students master the 3s and 4s, the last three groups—6s, 7s and 8s—should be very simple.

9. Teach the 6s, 7s and 8s

If you have taught all the groups in the order I have suggested, only three facts remain in the 6s, 7s and 8s which have not been taught. Please refer to the following page in which all previously taught groups have been crossed off of the Multiplication Facts Chart. The only remaining facts are 6×7, 6×8 and 7×8. 6×2 has already been learned along with the 2s facts. 6×3 has been learned with the 3s and so on. Since 6s, 7s and 8s are quite difficult for many kids to master, we used the process of elimination to learn them along with the easier groups.

10. Review, Reinforce and Reward

I think one of the reasons that phonics is so effective in language arts for most students is because whenever a student reads a book, review of what has been learned takes place. Review is extremely important in *Math Phonics™* as well. An occasional small reward is very valuable in keeping spirits up.

MULTIPLICATION FACTS CHART

squares

x	1s	2s	3s	4s	5s				9s	10s	11s	12s
x	**1**	**2**	**3**	**4**	**5**	**6**	**7**	**8**	**9**	**10**	**11**	**12**
1s **1**	1	2	3	4	5	6	7	8	9	10	11	12
2s **2**	2	4	6	8	10	12	14	16	18	20	22	24
3s **3**	3	6	9	12	15	18	21	24	27	30	33	36
4s **4**	4	8	12	16	20	24	28	32	36	40	44	48
5s **5**	5	10	15	20	25	30	35	40	45	50	55	60
6	6	12	18	24	30	36	(42)	(48)	54	60	66	72
7	7	14	21	28	35	(42)	49	(56)	63	70	77	84
8	8	16	24	32	40	(48)	(56)	64	72	80	88	96
9s **9**	9	18	27	36	45	54	63	72	81	90	99	108
10s **10**	10	20	30	40	50	60	70	80	90	100	110	120
11s **11**	11	22	33	44	55	66	77	88	99	110	121	132
12s **12**	12	24	36	48	60	72	84	96	108	120	132	144

9

LESSON PLAN 1

OBJECTIVE: Understanding the Concept of Multiplication. Students will understand the basic concept of multiplication by use of concrete examples. It is necessary for them to grasp *how* we find the answers to the multiplication facts before beginning to memorize them.

MATERIALS: Rectangular Array for 4s (page 13), pocket folders, parents' note (page 12)

INTRODUCTION: Tell students that multiplication is the shortcut to adding the same number several times. Show them one example in the room, such as floor tiles or perhaps rows and columns of windowpanes. Counting the number of desks in one row and multiplying by the number of rows would be another example.

Bring an example from home if necessary. An egg carton demonstrates 2 x 6. A checkerboard demonstrates 8 x 8.

DO: Use the Rectangular Array for 4s. Use a situation that might occur in students' lives such as bringing treats to school. The student can't remember how many are in the class, but the teacher did say that there are seven rows with four in each row. Tell students to use the Rectangular Array to find the correct answer. If necessary, explain that for 4 x 1, they should count the boxes in the first row, for 4 x 2, they count the boxes in the first two rows and so on.

Tell students to fill in all the correct answers in the right-hand column of blanks.

Explain that when the two numbers being multiplied are reversed, the answer is still the same.

NOTE: Emphasize that we use the multiplication tables to save time when adding the same number several times. Calculators can do this for us, but it is very important to be able to do this without help because we may not always have a calculator.

ASSIGNMENT: Students should find at least three examples of items in a rectangular array at home or on the way home. Small windowpanes in a large window or tiles in a floor are good examples. Sometimes newspaper advertisements show multiplication facts. For example, a light bulb ad might show two packs of light bulbs with four bulbs in each pack for an example of 4 x 2. Have them find more than three examples if they can.

CHALLENGE: Another way to visually present multiplication facts is to create a grid. Let vertical and horizontal lines represent the factors in the equation. Counting the points of intersection reveals the answer. For example: 2 x 3 would be drawn as two vertical lines crossing three hoizontal lines.

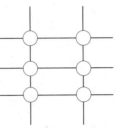

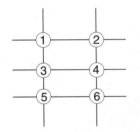

Now count the places where the lines cross.

Have students create grids for equations in the Rectangular Array for 4s.

TAKE-HOME: Give each student a pocket folder to keep Math Phonics materials in one place. Send home the note on page 12.

OPTIONAL: The Rectangular Array could be used as an art project. Students could color the array with two or more colors arranging the colors in various designs.

Small objects or stickers could be glued in each box. Mount on tagboard if necessary. Display around the room.

This art project is not an essential part of teaching this step, but some students benefit from manipulating objects to learn math concepts.

OPTIONAL: To stress the importance of learning to multiply, you could compare a calculator to a car. Cars are great when we need them, but most of the time we need to walk on our own. We teach our children to walk–we do not tell them, "You don't need to learn to walk–you can just use a car." It is a disadvantage not to be able to walk on your own. It's the same with a calculator. Calculators are great when we need them, but if a person can't multiply without one, it is a disadvantage.

OPTIONAL: Here is another student-related example. You have 50 cents to buy baseball cards. The ones you want cost 7 cents each. You live in a state where there is no sales tax. How many baseball cards can you buy? (Use the Base 10 Counting Chart on page 24.)

DEAR PARENTS,

Within the next few days our class will be starting a unit on multiplication using the Math Phonics™ program. This program is set up in such a way that your help is essential in order for your child to succeed in mastering the 91 math multiplication facts. Here are some of the things you can do to help:

1. Help your child find a good place to post the Travel Folders so that they will give a visual image to help master the facts on the folder. Some ideas would be on a mirror, the side of the fridge or on the wall near the light switch in the bedroom.

2. Verbally quiz your child from time to time, perhaps while you are fixing supper or driving in the car.

3. When your son or daughter has learned one group of facts, sign the appropriate space on the progress chart which will be sent home.

4. Once or twice a week, play one of the games your child has learned at school to reinforce the facts.

5. Once your child has learned several of the groups, review the first few groups once every week or two.

Please keep all the Math Phonics™ materials (worksheets, travel folders, progress charts, etc.) in the folder which your child has brought home. You may wish to purchase a clear plastic page protector and a dry-erase marker. Worksheets can be inserted in to the page protector, completed with the dry-erase marker and reused.

The Math Phonics™ program relies on teaching children patterns in the groups of multiplication facts. Visual images on wall posters, verbal and written review and lots of practice in the form of flash cards and games are ways to help children learn and recall these patterns.

Sincerely,

RECTANGULAR ARRAY FOR 4s

4 x 1 = ____

4 x 2 = ____

4 x 3 = ____

4 x 4 = ____

4 x 5 = ____

4 x 6 = ____

4 x 7 = ____

4 x 8 = ____

4 x 9 = ____

4 x 10 = ____

4 x 11 = ____

4 x 12 = ____

Student																									
Understands concept of multiplication																									
Found three examples of items in a rectangular array																									
Knows multiplication facts _ x 1																									
Knows multiplication facts _ x 2																									
Knows multiplication facts _ x 3																									
Knows multiplication facts _ x 4																									
Knows multiplication facts _ x 5																									
Knows multiplication facts _ x 6																									
Knows multiplication facts _ x 7																									
Knows multiplication facts _ x 8																									
Knows multiplication facts _ x 9																									
Knows multiplication facts _ x 10																									
Knows multiplication facts _ x 11																									
Knows multiplication facts _ x 12																									

LESSON PLAN 2

OBJECTIVE: Mastering the Perfect Squares. Students will start their memory work with the perfect squares—those facts in which the two numbers being multiplied are the same. They will use this group as a foundation for learning other groups and also for solving quadratic equations in algebra.

MATERIALS: Perfect Squares activity sheet (page 17), Practice Facts for Squares and 9s (page 18), Travel Folder for Squares (page 19), blank Multiplication Facts Chart (page 20)

INTRODUCTION: Spend about five minutes discussing the multiplication examples students have found. The squares group is good to teach first because most answers are spaced far apart on the number line. The only one in the teens is 16, the only one in the twenties is 25 and so on. These are easier to learn if they are learned first. Squares are very important in algebra because students need to know perfect squares in order to solve quadratic equations. Point out to students that 5 x 5 is five squared or five to the second power (5^2). This will make scientific notation a little easier later in school.

DO: Students will complete the Perfect Squares activity sheet. Explain that they are to connect the four dots under each multiplication fact. Then ask them to count the number of small squares in each large square and write that number in the blank space. Check to see that all answers are correct.

NOTE: Some students will have the squares answers memorized in just a few minutes while others will take much longer. This should not be a problem. There should be time for the slower students to catch up later. Tell them to practice at home.

ASSIGNMENT: Give students the Practice Facts for Squares and 9s sheet, fill in the squares answers and begin learning them. If there is time, have students chant the squares answers in order—column one of the Travel Folder for Squares. Have them chant column two, also. Students can study individually, as a group or they could pair off with a math study buddy.

OPTIONAL: You could enlarge and laminate the Travel Folder for Squares and post it in the classroom for students to study during free time.

TAKE-HOME: Give each student a Travel Folder for Squares and a vinyl page protector. Students could make their own Travel Folders on a piece of construction paper or an index card. Discuss where students could post the folder–above a light switch, on a mirror, side of the fridge, etc. Remind them to check with their parents before posting a folder.

Demonstrate how to fold the Travel Folder for Squares in thirds and study one column at a time. The right-hand column is to be used like a flash card–students ask themselves the facts in random order.

OPTIONAL: Perfect Squares activity sheet could be decorated as an art project.

CHALLENGE: Have the students write the answers to the perfect squares equations 0-11 in a vertical column. Ask them to study these numbers to see if they can detect any pattern in the sequence.

0	> 1
1	> 3
4	> 5
9	> 7
16	> 9
25	> 11
36	> 13
49	> 15
64	> 17
81	> 19
100	> 21
121	

OPTIONAL: Pass out the blank Multiplication Facts Chart and have students fill in the numbers 1-12 along the top row of boxes and the numbers 1-12 in the column of boxes at the left. Have students fill in the squares answers. For 5 x 5, have them find the 5 at the left and move to the right stopping at the box directly below the 5 in the top row. Write 25 in that box.

You might want to enlarge and laminate the blank Multiplication Facts Chart and post it in the room. Fill in answers as students study them.

You could hand out another blank Multiplication Facts Chart after all groups have been learned and have students fill it in as a quiz.

16

PERFECT SQUARES

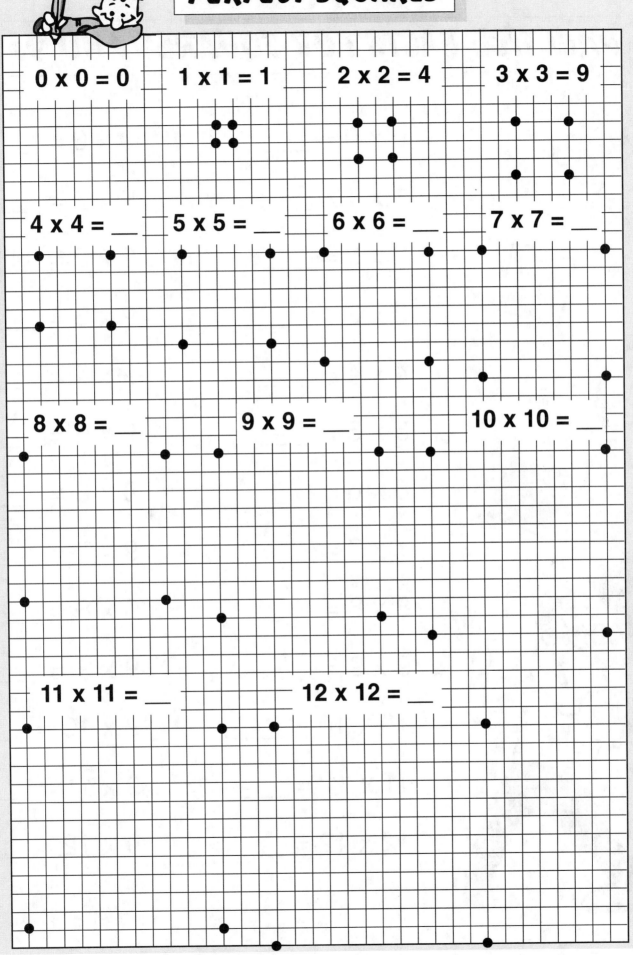

| 0 x 0 = 0 | 1 x 1 = 1 | 2 x 2 = 4 | 3 x 3 = 9 |

4 x 4 = __   5 x 5 = __   6 x 6 = __   7 x 7 = __

8 x 8 = __   9 x 9 = __   10 x 10 = __

11 x 11 = __   12 x 12 = __

PRACTICE FACTS FOR SQUARES AND 9s

0 x 0 = ___   9 x 0 = ___

1 x 1 = ___   9 x 1 = ___

2 x 2 = ___   9 x 2 = ___

3 x 3 = ___   9 x 3 = ___

4 x 4 = ___   9 x 4 = ___

5 x 5 = ___   9 x 5 = ___

6 x 6 = ___   9 x 6 = ___

7 x 7 = ___   9 x 7 = ___

8 x 8 = ___   9 x 8 = ___

9 x 9 = ___   9 x 9 = ___

10 x 10 = ___   9 x 10 = ___

11 x 11 = ___   9 x 11 = ___

12 x 12 = ___   9 x 12 = ___

Name _____

TRAVEL FOLDER FOR SQUARES

0	0 x 0 = 0	0 x 0
1	1 x 1 = 1	1 x 1
4	2 x 2 = 4	2 x 2
9	3 x 3 = 9	3 x 3
16	4 x 4 = 16	4 x 4
25	5 x 5 = 25	5 x 5
36	6 x 6 = 36	6 x 6
49	7 x 7 = 49	7 x 7
64	8 x 8 = 64	8 x 8
81	9 x 9 = 81	9 x 9
100	10 x 10 = 100	10 x 10
121	11 x 11 = 121	11 x 11
144	12 x 12 = 144	12 x 12

MULTIPLICATION FACTS CHART

x												

PERFECT SQUARES

Student																	
0 x 0																	
1 x 1																	
2 x 2																	
3 x 3																	
4 x 4																	
5 x 5																	
6 x 6																	
7 x 7																	
8 x 8																	
9 x 9																	
10 x 10																	
11 x 11																	
12 x 12																	

OBJECTIVE: Mastering the 9s Mulitplication Facts. Students will learn this difficult group by means of patterns. They will use this as another foundation group.

MATERIALS: Base 10 Counting Chart (page 24), Travel Folder for 9s (page 25), Worksheets for Squares and 9s (pages 26-28), Flash Cards for 9s (pages 29-38)

INTRODUCTION: Have the entire class chant the squares answers in order and the squares facts in order (columns one and two of the Travel Folder for Squares page 19). If students can say them without looking at any materials, have them raise their hands.

DO: Use an enlarged Base 10 Counting Chart or overhead projector. First circle the 9 because 9 x 1 = 9. Ask the class if they know the answer to 9 x 2. They should know this because they had to learn 9 + 9 = 18 in addition. Circle the 18. Some may know 9 x 3 = 27. If they do not, they should count nine more spaces from the 18 and circle 27. Ask if they can see the pattern as shown in the Optional on page 23. Some will see the pattern and know that the next answer is 36. Demonstrate that counting nine more spaces will give us 36. Continue counting by nine and circling the ninth number each time.

MEMORY TRICK: Another pattern is that the two digits in each answer will add up to 9 for all the answers up to 90. Here is a rhyme that students could learn:

When multiplying nine, keep this in mind:
Look at a number in the answer line.
Add the numerals together.
They will equal nine.

Have students practice naming the pairs of numbers that equal nine: 1 + 8, 2 + 7, 3 + 6 and 4 + 5. See page 28.

CHALLENGE: Ask students if they see any patterns in the answers. Some will probably observe that the number in the 10s column increases by one with each answer, and the number in the 1s column decreases by one with each answer. Also, 9s answers can be grouped in pairs: 18 and 81, 27 and 72, 36 and 63, 45 and 54.

OBSERVE: For the 9s facts from 9 x 2 to 9 x 10, the number in the 10s place of the answer is always one less than the number you are multiplying by 9. Since the two numbers added together equal nine, students can think of the answer in this way:

9 x 2 = ____ (Think: The answer is in the teens. 1 + 8 = 9 so the answer is 18.)
9 x 3 = ____ (Think: The answer is in the twenties. 2 + 7 = 9 so the answer is 27.)

TAKE-HOME: Give students a Travel Folder for 9s or have them make one on a piece of construction paper or index card. When students make their own study materials, they are learning at the same time. Travel Folders have large numerals which help students form a lasting visual image.

IN CLASS: If there is time, have students begin chanting the first two columns of the Travel Folder for 9s individually, as a group or in study buddy pairs.

ASSIGNMENT: Assign the Practice Facts for Squares and 9s (page 18) and Worksheets for Squares and 9s after a day or two of study.

OPTIONAL: Each student could have a small Base 10 Counting Chart and find the correct answers individually. Use a different counting chart when each new group is introduced, or give each student a page protector and marker to use. Clean off the page protector before starting a new group of multiplication facts.

Check that each student has the correct numbers circled, and then have them fill in the answers to the 9s facts on the Practice Facts for Squares and 9s (page 18).

9 x 0 = 0	9 x 7 = 63
9 x 1 = 9	9 x 8 = 72
9 x 2 = 18	9 x 9 = 81
9 x 3 = 27	9 x 10 = 90
9 x 4 = 36	9 x 11 = 99
9 x 5 = 45	9 x 12 = 108
9 x 6 = 54	

OPTIONAL: Worksheet A (page 39) for extra practice with the squares and 9s.

OPTIONAL: Have students fill in answers to the 9s on the blank Multiplication Facts Chart (page 20).

OPTIONAL: Worksheet B (page 40) to develop the students' awareness of whether a number is even or odd. Noticing whether a number is even or odd will help when reducing fractions and finding common denominators.

BASE 10 COUNTING CHART

1	2	3	4	5	6	7	8	9	10
11	12	13	14	15	16	17	18	19	20
21	22	23	24	25	26	27	28	29	30
31	32	33	34	35	36	37	38	39	40
41	42	43	44	45	46	47	48	49	50
51	52	53	54	55	56	57	58	59	60
61	62	63	64	65	66	67	68	69	70
71	72	73	74	75	76	77	78	79	80
81	82	83	84	85	86	87	88	89	90
91	92	93	94	95	96	97	98	99	100
101	102	103	104	105	106	107	108	109	110
111	112	113	114	115	116	117	118	119	120
121	122	123	124	125	126	127	128	129	130
131	132	133	134	135	136	137	138	139	140
141	142	143	144	145	146	147	148	149	150

Name _____

TRAVEL FOLDER FOR 9s

0	9 x 0 = 0	9 x 0
9	9 x 1 = 9	9 x 1
18	9 x 2 = 18	9 x 2
27	9 x 3 = 27	9 x 3
36	9 x 4 = 36	9 x 4
45	9 x 5 = 45	9 x 5
54	9 x 6 = 54	9 x 6
63	9 x 7 = 63	9 x 7
72	9 x 8 = 72	9 x 8
81	9 x 9 = 81	9 x 9
90	9 x 10 = 90	9 x 10
99	9 x 11 = 99	9 x 11
108	9 x 12 = 108	9 x 12

Name _____

1. **8 x 8** = ____

2. **10 x 10** = ____

3. **0 x 0** = ____

4. **9 x 2** = ____

5. **6 x 6** = ____

6. **9 x 6** = ____

7. **1 x 1** = ____

8. **5 x 5** = ____

9. **9 x 3** = ____

10. **4 x 4** = ____

11. **9 x 5** = ____

12. **9 x 0** = ____

13. **2 x 2** = ____

14. **9 x 9** = ____

15. **9 x 8** = ____

16. **7 x 7** = ____

17. **9 x 1** = ____

18. **3 x 3** = ____

19. **9 x 10** = ____

20. **9 x 0** = ____

26

WORKSHEET FOR SQUARES AND 9s

Count by 9s: 9, 18, 27, ____, ____, ____, ____, ____, ____, ____, ____, ____

21. **9 x 2** = ____   33. **9 x 6** = ____

22. **3 x 3** = ____   34. **7 x 7** = ____

23. **9 x 4** = ____   35. **9 x 8** = ____

24. **9 x 5** = ____   36. **8 x 8** = ____

25. **0 x 0** = ____   37. **9 x 9** = ____

26. **2 x 2** = ____   38. **10 x 10** = ____

27. **5 x 5** = ____   39. **9 x 1** = ____

28. **9 x 0** = ____   40. **9 x 10** = ____

29. **9 x 3** = ____   41. **11 x 11** = ____

30. **1 x 1** = ____   42. **12 x 12** = ____

31. **4 x 4** = ____   43. **9 x 11** = ____

32. **6 x 6** = ____   44. **9 x 12** = ____

WORKSHEET FOR SQUARES AND 9s

Remember these 9s addition facts:

```
   9          5          2
  +0         +4         +7
```

```
   8          4          1
  +1         +5         +8
```

```
   7          3          0
  +2         +6         +9
```

```
   6
  +3
```

Write the perfect squares.

0, 1, 4, 9, ___, ____, ____, ____, ____, ____, 100

$0 \times 0 =$	$0 \times 4 =$	$0 \times 8 =$	$0 \times 12 =$	$1 \times 4 =$
$0 \times 1 =$	$0 \times 5 =$	$0 \times 9 =$	$1 \times 1 =$	$1 \times 5 =$
$0 \times 2 =$	$0 \times 6 =$	$0 \times 10 =$	$1 \times 2 =$	$1 \times 6 =$
$0 \times 3 =$	$0 \times 7 =$	$0 \times 11 =$	$1 \times 3 =$	$1 \times 7 =$

$0 \times 0 = 0$	$0 \times 4 = 0$	$0 \times 8 = 0$	$0 \times 12 = 0$	$1 \times 4 = 4$
$0 \times 1 = 0$	$0 \times 5 = 0$	$0 \times 9 = 0$	$1 \times 1 = 1$	$1 \times 5 = 5$
$0 \times 2 = 0$	$0 \times 6 = 0$	$0 \times 10 = 0$	$1 \times 2 = 2$	$1 \times 6 = 6$
$0 \times 3 = 0$	$0 \times 7 = 0$	$0 \times 11 = 0$	$1 \times 3 = 3$	$1 \times 7 = 7$

3 x 3 =	2 x 9 =	2 x 5 =	1 x 12 =	1 x 8 =
3 x 4 =	2 x 10 =	2 x 6 =	2 x 2 =	1 x 9 =
3 x 5 =	2 x 11 =	2 x 7 =	2 x 3 =	1 x 10 =
3 x 6 =	2 x 12 =	2 x 8 =	2 x 4 =	1 x 11 =

$1 \times 8 = 8$

$1 \times 9 = 9$

$1 \times 10 = 10$

$1 \times 11 = 11$

$1 \times 12 = 12$

$2 \times 2 = 4$

$2 \times 3 = 6$

$2 \times 4 = 8$

$2 \times 5 = 10$

$2 \times 6 = 12$

$2 \times 7 = 14$

$2 \times 8 = 16$

$2 \times 9 = 18$

$2 \times 10 = 20$

$2 \times 11 = 22$

$2 \times 12 = 24$

$3 \times 3 = 9$

$3 \times 4 = 12$

$3 \times 5 = 15$

$3 \times 6 = 18$

5 x 6 =	4 x 10 =	4 x 6 =	3 x 11 =	3 x 7 =
5 x 7 =	4 x 11 =	4 x 7 =	3 x 12 =	3 x 8 =
5 x 8 =	4 x 12 =	4 x 8 =	4 x 4 =	3 x 9 =
5 x 9 =	5 x 5 =	4 x 9 =	4 x 5 =	3 x 10 =

$3 \times 7 = 21$	$3 \times 11 = 33$	$4 \times 6 = 24$	$4 \times 10 = 40$	$5 \times 6 = 30$
$3 \times 8 = 24$	$3 \times 12 = 36$	$4 \times 7 = 28$	$4 \times 11 = 44$	$5 \times 7 = 35$
$3 \times 9 = 27$	$4 \times 4 = 16$	$4 \times 8 = 32$	$4 \times 12 = 48$	$5 \times 8 = 40$
$3 \times 10 = 30$	$4 \times 5 = 20$	$4 \times 9 = 36$	$5 \times 5 = 25$	$5 \times 9 = 45$

$8 \times 8 =$	$7 \times 9 =$	$6 \times 11 =$	$6 \times 7 =$	$5 \times 10 =$
$8 \times 9 =$	$7 \times 10 =$	$6 \times 12 =$	$6 \times 8 =$	$5 \times 11 =$
$8 \times 10 =$	$7 \times 11 =$	$7 \times 7 =$	$6 \times 9 =$	$5 \times 12 =$
$8 \times 11 =$	$7 \times 12 =$	$7 \times 8 =$	$6 \times 10 =$	$6 \times 6 =$

5 x 10 = 50	6 x 7 = 42	6 x 11 = 66	7 x 9 = 63	8 x 8 = 64
5 x 11 = 55	6 x 8 = 48	6 x 12 = 72	7 x 10 = 70	8 x 9 = 72
5 x 12 = 60	6 x 9 = 54	7 x 7 = 49	7 x 11 = 77	8 x 10 = 80
6 x 6 = 36	6 x 10 = 60	7 x 8 = 56	7 x 12 = 84	8 x 11 = 88

		11 × 11 =	9 × 12 =	8 × 12 =
		11 × 12 =	10 × 10 =	9 × 9 =
		12 × 12 =	10 × 11 =	9 × 10 =
			10 × 12 =	9 × 11 =

8 × 12 = 96	9 × 12 = 108	11 × 11 = 121		
9 × 9 = 81	10 × 10 = 100	11 × 12 = 132		
9 × 10 = 90	10 × 11 = 110	12 × 12 = 144		
9 × 11 = 99	10 × 12 = 120			

SQUARES AND 9s

Directions: For each pair of multiplication facts, circle the one whose answer is larger. If they are the same, circle both.

1. **5 x 5** or **9 x 3**   7. **0 x 0** or **9 x 0**

2. **4 x 4** or **9 x 9**   8. **9 x 4** or **6 x 6**

3. **3 x 3** or **9 x 0**   9. **9 x 1** or **3 x 3**

4. **2 x 2** or **9 x 1**   10. **9 x 11** or **10 x 10**

5. **6 x 6** or **9 x 3**   11. **9 x 12** or **11 x 11**

6. **7 x 7** or **9 x 5**   12. **9 x 2** or **5 x 5**

13. The Bixby brothers each have a small bean garden. Bob planted 10 rows with 10 plants in each row. Bubba planted 9 rows with 11 plants in each row. Which brother had a larger number of bean plants?

14. Their sister, Betty, picked beans for them. She picked 3 beans from each of Bob's plants and 1 bean from each of Bubba's plants. How many beans did she pick in all?

15. Betty will be canning beans. She has 9 jars to fill. Each jar holds 9 cups of beans and 1 cup of water. How many cups of beans will she need?

16. The Bixbys canned 9 jars of beans every day for a week. How many jars of beans were canned by the end of the week?

17. Next to the bean garden, the Bixbys have 2 strawberry patches. One patch has 4 rows with 9 plants in each row. The other has 5 rows with 5 plants in each row. What is the total number of plants in these 2 patches?

18. The Bixby's entire garden is 12 feet long and 12 feet wide. How many square feet are in the entire garden?

CHALLENGE: Write the names of all the foods you can think of that begin with an *S* or a *B*. If you were on a game show and you got nine points for each correct answer, how many points would you have?

SQUARES AND 9s

Directions: Choose two colors. Use them to color this design.

Color 1: _____ for sections where the answer is an odd number (ends in 1, 3, 5, 7 or 9)

Color 2: _____ for sections where the answer is an even number (ends in 0, 2, 4, 6 or 8)

7 x 7 =

8 x 8 =

9 x 5 =

9 x 4 =

3 x 3 =

9 x 7 =

9 x 9 =

9 x 6 =

9 x 1 =

0 x 0 =

9 x 2 =

5 x 5 =

11 x 11 =

2 x 2 =

9 x 11 =

9 x 3 =

9 x 5 =

6 x 6 =

1 x 1 =

9s

Student																				
9 x 0																				
9 x 1																				
9 x 2																				
9 x 3																				
9 x 4																				
9 x 5																				
9 x 6																				
9 x 7																				
9 x 8																				
9 x 9																				
9 x 10																				
9 x 11																				
9 x 12																				

LESSON PLAN 4

OBJECTIVE: Mastering the Facts for 0s, 1s and 2s. (The facts for 0s and 1s can be tricky. Children often get confused by the differences in multiplying by 0 or 1 and *adding* 0 or 1. It is often helpful for them to start with larger numbers and work down to 1 and 0. For example: 5 x 2 =, 5 x 1 =, 5 x 0 =.) Students will understand the difference between adding 0 or 1 to a number and multiplying by 0 or 1. The facts for 2s are introduced here and developed further in Lesson Plan 5.

INTRODUCTION: Have students chant answers and complete facts for squares and 9s.

DO: On the board, write 5 x 2, 5 x 1 and 5 x 0. Have 10 students stand at the front of the classroom in two rows of five each. Explain that 5 x 2 and 2 x 5 both equal 10. Have five students sit down. We now have 5 x 1 and 1 x 5 and the answer is 5. Ask students how this is different from 5 + 1. Have the last five students sit down. Tell students that we now have zero rows with five students in each row. That means 5 x 0 = 0. Also, 0 x 5 = 0. How is this different from 5 + 0? (Example: Five students are playing basketball. No one joins them. There are still five playing. That shows 5 + 0 = 5.)

CHALLENGE: Ask students to make up a rule for multiplying by zero and by one. The rules should be something like this:

Any number times zero equals zero.

Any number times one equals that same number.

OPTIONAL: Fill in 0s and 1s on the blank Multiplication Facts Chart (page 20).

MATERIALS: Practice Facts for 0s, 1s and 2s (page 45); five bowls and 10 counters such as pennies; Student's Math Phonics™ Progress Chart and Teacher's Math Phonics™ Progress Chart (pages 43-44); Flash Cards for 0s, 1s and 2s (pages 29-38)

ASSIGNMENT: Use the Practice Facts for 0s, 1s and 2s. Have students fill in the answers to the 0s and 1s. Twos will be taught in Lesson Plan 5.

There is no Travel Folder for these groups because most students will learn them with very little effort. Do not chant answers for 0s and 1s because it would be boring. Students could chant the facts in order but only once or twice.

Give each student a Math Phonics™ Progess Chart with spaces to be signed by a classmate or parent. Once a week they should bring the chart to you so you can keep track of their progress on your Teacher's Math Phonics™ Progess Chart.

OPTIONAL: If students seem confused by the concept of multiplying by zero, use the five bowls and 10 counters. Put two counters in each bowl. This demonstrates 5 x 2, and we can have a student count the 10 pennies. Remove one penny from each bowl. We now have five bowls with one penny in each bowl. 5 x 1 = 5. Remove the last penny from each bowl. There are now five bowls with zero pennies in each bowl. 5 x 0 = 0. One of the students might say that there are five bowls, but we are not counting bowls. We are counting pennies. If we had 10 bowls and all were empty, we would still have zero pennies.

Name _____

STUDENT'S MATH PHONICS™ PROGRESS CHART

	Say facts in order	Say facts not in order	**Practice Facts** How many right?	**Worksheet** How many right?
Squares				
9s				
0s				
1s				
2s				
10s				
11s				
12s				
3s				
4s				
5s				
6s				
7s				
8s				
Assessment	X	X	X	X

Have a parent or classmate sign these spaces when you can say them correctly.

43

TEACHER'S MATH PHONICS™ PROGRESS CHART

Name	Squares and 9s	0s, 1s and 2s	10s, 11s and 12s	3s, 4s and 5s	6s, 7s and 8s	Assessment

Write the date when the student has mastered each group.

TLC10069 Copyright © Teaching & Learning Company, Carthage, IL 62321

Name _____

PRACTICE FACTS FOR 0s, 1s AND 2s

0 x 0 = ___	1 x 0 = ___	2 x 0 = ___
0 x 1 = ___	1 x 1 = ___	2 x 1 = ___
0 x 2 = ___	1 x 2 = ___	2 x 2 = ___
0 x 3 = ___	1 x 3 = ___	2 x 3 = ___
0 x 4 = ___	1 x 4 = ___	2 x 4 = ___
0 x 5 = ___	1 x 5 = ___	2 x 5 = ___
0 x 6 = ___	1 x 6 = ___	2 x 6 = ___
0 x 7 = ___	1 x 7 = ___	2 x 7 = ___
0 x 8 = ___	1 x 8 = ___	2 x 8 = ___
0 x 9 = ___	1 x 9 = ___	2 x 9 = ___
0 x 10 = ___	1 x 10 = ___	2 x 10 = ___
0 x 11 = ___	1 x 11 = ___	2 x 11 = ___
0 x 12 = ___	1 x 12 = ___	2 x 12 = ___

0s AND 1s

0 x 0																	
0 x 1																	
0 x 2																	
0 x 3																	
0 x 4																	
0 x 5																	
0 x 6																	
0 x 7																	
0 x 8																	
0 x 9																	
0 x 10																	
0 x 11																	
0 x 12																	
1 x 0																	
1 x 1																	
1 x 2																	
1 x 3																	
1 x 4																	
1 x 5																	
1 x 6																	
1 x 7																	
1 x 8																	
1 x 9																	
1 x 10																	
1 x 11																	
1 x 12																	

LESSON PLAN 5

OBJECTIVE: Mastering the 2s Group. Students will next learn the group of facts consisting of two times each number. They will learn the relationship between doubles in addition (3 + 3 = 6, 4 + 4 = 8) and this 2s group in multiplication (3 x 2 = 6, 4 x 2 = 8).

MATERIALS: Base 10 Counting Chart (page 24); Worksheet for 0s, 1s and 2s (page 49); instructions for games (page 48); Flash Cards for 2s (pages 29-38); Practice Facts for 0s, 1s and 2s (page 45)

INTRODUCTION: Review the concepts of multiplying by zero and by one. Chant the facts in order for 0s, 1s, 9s and squares. Review the rules for multiplying by 9s, if necessary.

DO: Use the Base 10 Counting Chart or over-head projector as described in the section on 9s. Since this group is the 2s, the students will circle the two for 2 x 1, the 4 for 2 x 2 and so on up to 24. Check to be sure that each student has the correct numbers circled. Have students fill in the correct answers to the 2s facts on the Practice Facts for 0s, 1s and 2s. There is no Travel Folder for 0s, 1s and 2s, but the Practice Facts sheet can be posted if some of the students want to do so. It is probably not necessary to chant the 2s answers but helpful to chant the 2s facts in order.

ASSIGNMENT: Worksheet for 0s, 1s and 2s could be an in-class or take-home assignment.

TAKE-HOME: Have students add flash cards for the 2s facts to the ones that have previously been studied. Give a brief explanation of the game instructions for students to use at home for drill. Playing games during class is generally not a very efficient way to use time.

OPTIONAL: Fill in the 2s answers on the blank Multiplication Facts Chart (page 20). Use any extra minutes of class time to have students count off by 2s, 9s or answers of any other group of facts that you might be studying.

CHALLENGE: Ask students to make up a rule to help them remember the 2s. Some possibilities would be that all the answers are even numbers, answers are like counting by 2s or answers are the same as the doubles in addition.

OPTIONAL: Worksheet D (page 51)—Another look at evens and odds. Be sure students notice that the only way to get an odd number in the 1s place of an answer is to multiply odd times odd.

OPTIONAL: Worksheet C (page 50)—Multiplying Two Columns. For these two-digit problems, there will be no carrying. Do the first three problems in class using the Base 10 Counting Chart.

$$21 \times 2$$

Count 21 spaces on the counting chart, then another 21. The result is 42. The same answer can be found by multiplying 2 x 1 for the 1s-place numeral and 2 x 2 for the 10s-place numeral. Do numbers 2 and 3 the same way. (Note: This is a good preview for the 10s, 11s and 12s.)

TLC10069 Copyright © Teaching & Learning Company, Carthage, IL 62321

MATH PHONICS™ GAMES

Try making a few changes in favorite games such as these:

TRIVIAL PURSUIT™: Replace the question cards with math flash cards. Play the game according to the rules.

SCATTERGORIES™: Play the game according to the rules. When the time comes to add each person's score, let each correct answer count three if students are studying the 3s. Do the same for 4s, 5s or any other multiplication group.

RACKO™: This game has cards numbered from 1 to 60. Use these cards in the way that the Math Pack (page 66) is used. If students are working on 7s, pull out the cards which are multiples of seven. Have students mix them up, put them in order, turn up a card and say the multiplication fact which goes with that card.

CALENDARS: Point out to students that the numbers directly below the seven on a calendar are multiples of seven (7, 14, 21, 28). Each time they look at a calendar, they can practice the first four 7s facts. Old calendars can be used like a Base 10 Counting Chart. Students can practice circling every third number or every fourth number.

PLAYING CARD FLASH CARDS

Remove face cards for all games.

TWO-PLAYER SPEED

1. Deal out all cards to two players.
2. On the count of three, both players turn up the top card.
3. The two numbers on the cards make up the multiplication fact.
4. The first person to call out the correct answer wins both cards.
5. Use the Multiplication Facts Chart to check the answers.
6. Game ends when one player wins all the cards.
7. If players are evenly matched and it seems that the game will never end, set a time limit and the winner is the person with the most cards at the end of that time period.

TWO-PLAYER SPEED VARIATION

1. Follow steps for Two-Player Speed except for #4.
2. Players take turns calling out the correct answer.
3. Players who answer correctly keep the cards.

FLASH CARDS FOR ONE GROUP

1. An example using 9s: Turn up a nine and leave it turned up during the game.
2. Turn up the other cards one at a time.
3. Put that card with the nine to form a math fact.
4. Players keep the card when they answer correctly.
5. This can be played as a one or two-player game, speed or speed variation.

FLASH CARDS FOR SQUARES

1. Turn up cards one at a time.
2. Square the number that was turned up.
3. Give the answer to that square. (Example: 5 was turned up. 25 is the answer.)
4. Players keep the card when they answer correctly.
5. This can be a one or two-player game, speed or speed variation.

Name _____

WORKSHEET FOR 0s, 1s AND 2s

1. **1 x 10** = ___
2. **2 x 1** = ___
3. **2 x 0** = ___
4. **1 x 9** = ___
5. **6 x 0** = ___
6. **3 x 1** = ___
7. **4 x 2** = ___
8. **9 x 0** = ___
9. **7 x 1** = ___
10. **8 x 2** = ___
11. **3 x 0** = ___
12. **9 x 2** = ___
13. **5 x 0** = ___
14. **6 x 2** = ___

15. **4 x 0** = ___
16. **5 x 1** = ___
17. **1 x 1** = ___
18. **4 x 1** = ___
19. **6 x 1** = ___
20. **8 x 1** = ___
21. **2 x 2** = ___
22. **2 x 3** = ___
23. **2 x 5** = ___
24. **2 x 7** = ___
25. **1 x 0** = ___
26. **7 x 0** = ___
27. **0 x 0** = ___
28. **3 x 2** = ___

Count by 2s: 2, 4, 6, ___, ___, ___, ___, ___, ___, ___, ___, ___

Count by 9s: 9, 18, 27, ___, ___, ___, ___, ___, ___, ___, ___, ___

Perfect Squares: 0, 1, 4, 9, ___, ___, ___, ___, ___, ___, ___, ___, ___

TRY THIS

Use the Base 10 Counting Chart to find the missing numbers.

Count by 3s: 3, 6, 9, 12, ___, ___, ___, ___, ___, ___, ___, ___

Count by 4s: 4, 8, 12, ___, ___, ___, ___, ___, ___, ___, ___, ___

Count by 5s: 5, 10, 15, ___, ___, ___, ___, ___, ___, ___, ___, ___

MULTIPLYING TWO COLUMNS

1. 21
    x 2
    42

2. 21
    x 3
    63

3. 10
    x 3
    30

4. 11
    x 4
    44

5. 33
    x 2
    66

6. 11
    x 2
    22

7. 10
    x 5
    50

8. 12
    x 3
    38

9. 32
    x 1
    32

10. 13
    x 2
    26

11. 31
    x 2
    62

12. 24
    x 2
    46

13. 35
    x 1
    35

14. 12
    x 2
    24

15. 11
    x 6
    66

16. 22
    x 3
    66

17. 33
    x 1
    33

18. 11
    x 6
    66

19. 20
    x 3
    60

20. 33
    x 3
    99

21. 16
    x 1
    16

22. 10
    x 6
    60

23. 10
    x 9
    90

24. 12
    x 4
    48

25. 11
    x 9
    99

26. 40
    x 2
    80

27. 11
    x 3
    33

28. 10
    x 8
    80

29. 30
    x 3
    90

30. 45
    x 1
    45

31. 11
    x 8
    88

32. 22
    x 2
    44

33. 67
    x 1
    67

34. 34
    x 2
    68

35. 42
    x 2
    84

CHALLENGE: The Base 10 Counting Chart is a number line. A ruler is a number line. List all of the other number lines you can find or think of in your home, car or elsewhere in the world. (Note: A number line can be circular.) If you were working for a company which paid you $6.00 for each number line you had on your list, how much money would you have?

Name _____

EVENS AND ODDS

Directions: Write each math fact from the list below *with its answer* in the correct column.
Example: 2 x 4 = 8 goes in the Even x Even column because 2 and 4 are even numbers. Three have been done for you.

1 x 1, 2 x 2, 4 x 4, 5 x 5, 6 x 6, 7 x 7, 8 x 8, 9 x 9, 10 x 10, 11 x 11, 12 x 12
9 x 1, 9 x 2, 9 x 3, 9 x 4, 9 x 5, 9 x 6, 9 x 7, 9 x 8, 9 x 10, 9 x 11, 9 x 12
2 x 1, 2 x 3, 2 x 5, 2 x 6, 2 x 7, 2 x 8, 2 x 10, 2 x 11, 2 x 12

Even x Even	Odd x Odd	Even x Odd
2 x 4 = 8	3 x 3 = 9	2 x 9 = 18

Directions: Circle the correct word in each sentence.

1. An even number times an even number always equals an (even, odd) number.

2. An odd number times an odd number always equals an (even, odd) number.

3. An even number times an odd number always equals an (even, odd) number.

CHALLENGE: If a quarter weighs 9 grams, how much would $3.00 in quarters weigh?

EXTRA CHALLENGE: Hot dogs come in packs of 10. Hot dog buns come in packs of 8. What is the smallest number of hot dogs and buns you would have to buy in order to have the same number of hot dogs and buns?

51

2s

2 x 0																				
2 x 1																				
2 x 2																				
2 x 3																				
2 x 4																				
2 x 5																				
2 x 6																				
2 x 7																				
2 x 8																				
2 x 9																				
2 x 10																				
2 x 11																				
2 x 12																				

OBJECTIVE: Mastering the 10s, 11s and 12s Groups. Students will learn the 10s and 11s by observing the patterns in the answers. They will learn 12s and use those facts in problems involving feet and inches and dozens of objects.

MATERIALS: Base 10 Counting Chart (page 24); Practice Facts and Worksheet for 10s, 11s and 12s (pages 55-56); Math Phonics™ certificate (page 96) and parents' Note 1 (page 54); Flash Cards for 10s, 11s and 12s (pages 29-38); Worksheets (pages 57-58)

INTRODUCTION: 10s and 11s are fairly easy to teach because of the repetitive pattern of the answers. 12s are a little harder. Some teachers do not require memorization of the 12s, but they come in handy for converting from feet to inches and working with hours on a clock and items counted by dozens and months of the year.

DO: Hand out a certificate or small prize to all students as they memorize these first eight groups of facts.

BREAK: If some students need more time to memorize facts, take a break here and study an unrelated chapter such as measurements, geometry or the metric system. Have students continue to practice at home if they haven't learned all the groups. Those who have learned the facts should review from time to time so they will not forget what they have learned.
Send home parents' Note 1. Record students' progress on Teacher's Math Phonics™ Progress Chart (page 44).

OPTIONAL: Fill in 10s, 11s and 12s on the blank Multiplication Facts Chart (page 20).

OPTIONAL: Worksheet E—Hexagon Problems. Self-explanatory.

DO: Teach the 10s using the Base 10 Counting Chart as described in the section on 9s. Give each student a Practice Facts for 10s, 11s and 12s. Have students fill in the answers for 10s. Ask students to think of a simple rule for multiplying by 10.
Rule: When multiplying a number by 10, add a 0 to the right of the number.
Repeat the process for 11s.
Rule: When multiplying a one-digit number by 11, write that digit in the 10s place and in the 1s place of the answer.

CHALLENGE: Repeat the process for 12s. Ask students if they can see a pattern for multiplying by 12. One pattern is that the 10s increase by one, while the 1s number increases by two each time. Here's another good shortcut to find 12 times a number. A good example is 11 x 7.

$$11 \times 7 = 77 \quad \text{To find } 12 \times 7, \text{ add another group of 7.}$$
$$\frac{+7}{12 \times 7 = 84}$$

PRACTICE: Have students chant these three groups of facts in order. Chant just the answers to the 12s if necessary. Add flash cards for these three groups.

ASSIGNMENT: Worksheet for 10s, 11s and 12s. This could be assigned after a day or two of practice.

OPTIONAL: Worksheet F—Multiplying by 10s and 100s. To multiply 4 x 100, we could add 100 four times since multiplication is the short way of adding the same number several times.

$$4 \times 100 = 100 + 100 + 100 + 100 = 400$$

Shortcut Rule: To multiply a number by 100, add two 0s to that number. (Write 4 and 00.)

Dear Parents,

Our class has been working on multiplication facts for two weeks. Thank you very much for the help you have given at home. Your child has mastered these groups of facts: _____

Your child needs to learn these facts as soon as possible: _____

For the next two weeks, we will be studying a unit on _____. During that time, your child still needs to review and practice these first eight groups. Use the flash cards and games. Please keep them in the pocket folder and help your child with them at least two or three times a week.

After we finish the unit above, we will return to multiplication for another two week unit. Then later in the year, we will have periodic reviews. I want the children to practice at home at least once a week for the rest of the year. The facts are extremely important for the children to master before they go on to new math material.

Once again, thank you for helping at home.

Sincerely,

Dear Parents,

We have now finished our last two weeks of *Math Phonics™–Multiplication*. Your child still needs to spend some more time on these groups: _____

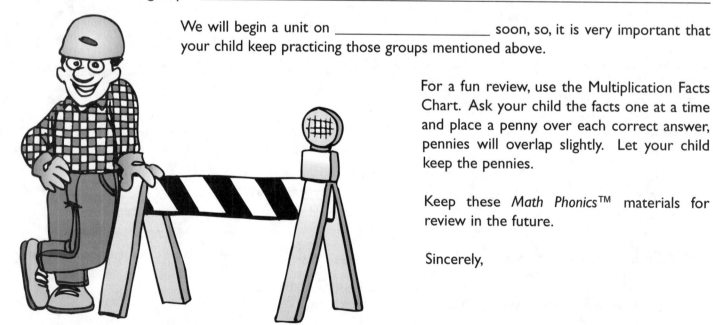

We will begin a unit on _____ soon, so, it is very important that your child keep practicing those groups mentioned above.

For a fun review, use the Multiplication Facts Chart. Ask your child the facts one at a time and place a penny over each correct answer, pennies will overlap slightly. Let your child keep the pennies.

Keep these *Math Phonics™* materials for review in the future.

Sincerely,

54

Name _____

10 x 0 = ___	11 x 0 = ___	12 x 0 = ___
10 x 1 = ___	11 x 1 = ___	12 x 1 = ___
10 x 2 = ___	11 x 2 = ___	12 x 2 = ___
10 x 3 = ___	11 x 3 = ___	12 x 3 = ___
10 x 4 = ___	11 x 4 = ___	12 x 4 = ___
10 x 5 = ___	11 x 5 = ___	12 x 5 = ___
10 x 6 = ___	11 x 6 = ___	12 x 6 = ___
10 x 7 = ___	11 x 7 = ___	12 x 7 = ___
10 x 8 = ___	11 x 8 = ___	12 x 8 = ___
10 x 9 = ___	11 x 9 = ___	12 x 9 = ___
10 x 10 = ___	11 x 10 = ___	12 x 10 = ___
10 x 11 = ___	11 x 11 = ___	12 x 11 = ___
10 x 12 = ___	11 x 12 = ___	12 x 12 = ___

Name _____

WORKSHEET FOR 10s, 11s AND 12s

1. **6 x 10** = ___

2. **2 x 11** = ___

3. **2 x 10** = ___

4. **11 x 9** = ___

5. **10 x 0** = ___

6. **3 x 11** = ___

7. **4 x 12** = ___

8. **9 x 10** = ___

9. **0 x 12** = ___

10. **8 x 12** = ___

11. **3 x 10** = ___

12. **9 x 12** = ___

13. **0 x 11** = ___

14. **6 x 12** = ___

15. **4 x 10** = ___

16. **5 x 11** = ___

17. **1 x 10** = ___

18. **4 x 11** = ___

19. **7 x 11** = ___

20. **8 x 11** = ___

21. **7 x 10** = ___

22. **7 x 12** = ___

23. **8 x 10** = ___

24. **11 x 12** = ___

25. **11 x 6** = ___

26. **5 x 10** = ___

27. **0 x 10** = ___

28. **3 x 12** = ___

Count by 2s: 2, 4, 6, ___, ___, ___, ___, ___, ___, ___, ___, ___

Count by 9s: 9, 18, 27, ___, ___, ___, ___, ___, ___, ___, ___, ___

Perfect Squares: 0, 1, 4, 9, ___, ___, ___, ___, ___, ___, ___, ___, ___

TRY THIS

Use the Base 10 Counting Chart to find the missing numbers.

Count by 3s: 3, 6, 9, 12, ___, ___, ___, ___, ___, ___, ___, ___

Count by 4s: 4, 8, 12, ___, ___, ___, ___, ___, ___, ___, ___, ___

Count by 5s: 5, 10, 15, ___, ___, ___, ___, ___, ___, ___, ___, ___

56

HEXAGON PROBLEMS

Directions: Multiply the number in the center times each number in an adjoining smaller hexagon. Put each answer in the outer hexagon. Two have been done for you.

1.

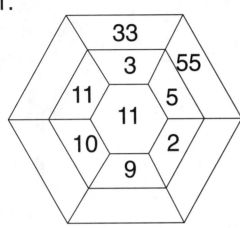

33 3 55
11 5
11
10 2
9

4.

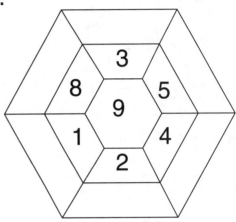

3
8 5
9
1 4
2

2.

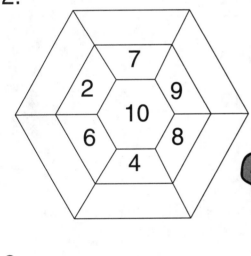

7
2 9
10
6 8
4

5.

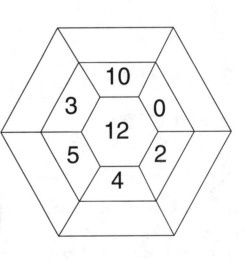

10
3 0
12
5 2
4

3.

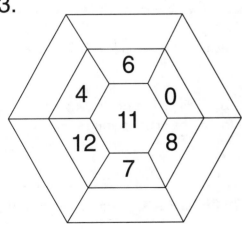

6
4 0
11
12 8
7

6.

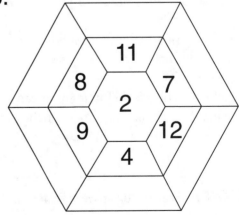

11
8 7
2
9 12
4

MULTIPLYING BY 10s AND 100s

Directions: Fill in the blanks.

1. **5 x 10 =** _____

2. **3 x 10 =** _____

3. **7 x 10 =** _____

4. **4 x 10 =** _____

5. **8 x 10 =** _____

6. **4 x 100 =** _____

7. **7 x 100 =** _____

8. **8 x 100 =** _____

9. **10 x 10 =** _____

10. **11 x 10 =** _____

11. **12 x 10 =** _____

12. **100 x 2 =** _____

13. **13 x 10 =** _____

14. **15 x 10 =** _____

15. **22 x 10 =** _____

16. **33 x 10 =** _____

17. **65 x 100 =** _____

18. **72 x 10 =** _____

19. **132 x 10 =** _____

20. **221 x 10 =** _____

Directions: Show your work. Label answers.

21. The Sharp family runs a clothing store. They are buying tube socks in packs containing 10 pairs of socks. If there are 9 packs in each carton, how many pairs of socks are in each carton?

22. The rack for shoes holds 23 rows. If there are 10 shoes in each row, how many shoes are on the rack?

23. The Sharps need to know the width of the display window in inches. If the window is 9 feet wide, how wide is it in inches?

24. List all the articles of clothing you can think of that begin with S. Each article of clothing needs 3 inches of space on a shelf. How many inches of space will you need for all the articles you listed?

CHALLENGE: State your answer to #24 in feet and inches.

EXTRA CHALLENGE: Convert your answer to metric.

10s, 11s AND 12s

Student

10 x 0																						
10 x 1																						
10 x 2																						
10 x 3																						
10 x 4																						
10 x 5																						
10 x 6																						
10 x 7																						
10 x 8																						
10 x 9																						
10 x 10																						
10 x 11																						
10 x 12																						
11 x 0																						
11 x 1																						
11 x 2																						
11 x 3																						
11 x 4																						
11 x 5																						
11 x 6																						
11 x 7																						
11 x 8																						
11 x 9																						
11 x 10																						
11 x 11																						
11 x 12																						
12 x 0																						
12 x 1																						
12 x 2																						
12 x 3																						
12 x 4																						
12 x 5																						
12 x 6																						
12 x 7																						
12 x 8																						
12 x 9																						
12 x 10																						
12 x 11																						
12 x 12																						

OBJECTIVE: Mastering the 5s Facts. Students will learn the 5s multiplication facts by observing the patterns in the answers. They will relate these facts to what they are learning about telling time and counting money.

MATERIALS: Base 10 Counting Chart (page 24); Rectangular Array for 5s (page 61); Practice Facts for 3s, 4s and 5s (page 62); Flash Cards for 5s (pages 29-38)

ASSIGNMENT: Add flash cards for 5, and have students begin chanting the facts in order. Assign the Rectangular Array for 5s if necessary.

INTRODUCTION: Have students chant all previous groups in order. Have students count by 5s to 100. Remind them that they learned this for telling time and counting money. Use the Base10 Counting Chart as described in the lesson on 9s. Next, students should fill in the answers to the 5s on the Practice Facts for 3s, 4s and 5s.

CHALLENGE: Set up the 5s on the chalkboard in this manner:

5 x 1 = 5	5 x 2 = 10
5 x 3 = 15	5 x 4 = 20
5 x 5 = 25	5 x 6 = 30
5 x 7 = 35	5 x 8 = 40
5 x 9 = 45	5 x 10 = 50
5 x 11 = 55	5 x 12 = 60

Ask students what patterns they see. What you want them to notice is:

Rule: Five times an odd number always ends in five, and five times an even number always ends in zero.

Also, for five times an even number, take half of that even number and put that number in the 10s place of the answer.

OPTIONAL: Fill in the 5s on the blank Multiplication Facts Chart.

OPTIONAL: A large clock face is an excellent visual aid for teaching the 5s. The 12 numbers representing hours should be on the face of the clock. On the outer edge of the clock would be the multiples of five representing minutes. Thus, near the three would be 15 for 15 minutes and 3 x 5 = 15. Near the nine would be 45 for 45 minutes and 5 x 9 = 45. Students can use their knowledge of telling time to help them learn the 5s.

RECTANGULAR ARRAY FOR 5s

5 x 1 = ___

5 x 2 = ___

5 x 3 = ___

5 x 4 = ___

5 x 5 = ___

5 x 6 = ___

5 x 7 = ___

5 x 8 = ___

5 x 9 = ___

5 x 10 = ___

5 x 11 = ___

5 x 12 = ___

61

PRACTICE FACTS FOR 3s, 4s AND 5s

3 x 0 = ___	4 x 0 = ___	5 x 0 = ___
3 x 1 = ___	4 x 1 = ___	5 x 1 = ___
3 x 2 = ___	4 x 2 = ___	5 x 2 = ___
3 x 3 = ___	4 x 3 = ___	5 x 3 = ___
3 x 4 = ___	4 x 4 = ___	5 x 4 = ___
3 x 5 = ___	4 x 5 = ___	5 x 5 = ___
3 x 6 = ___	4 x 6 = ___	5 x 6 = ___
3 x 7 = ___	4 x 7 = ___	5 x 7 = ___
3 x 8 = ___	4 x 8 = ___	5 x 8 = ___
3 x 9 = ___	4 x 9 = ___	5 x 9 = ___
3 x 10 = ___	4 x 10 = ___	5 x 10 = ___
3 x 11 = ___	4 x 11 = ___	5 x 11 = ___
3 x 12 = ___	4 x 12 = ___	5 x 12 = ___

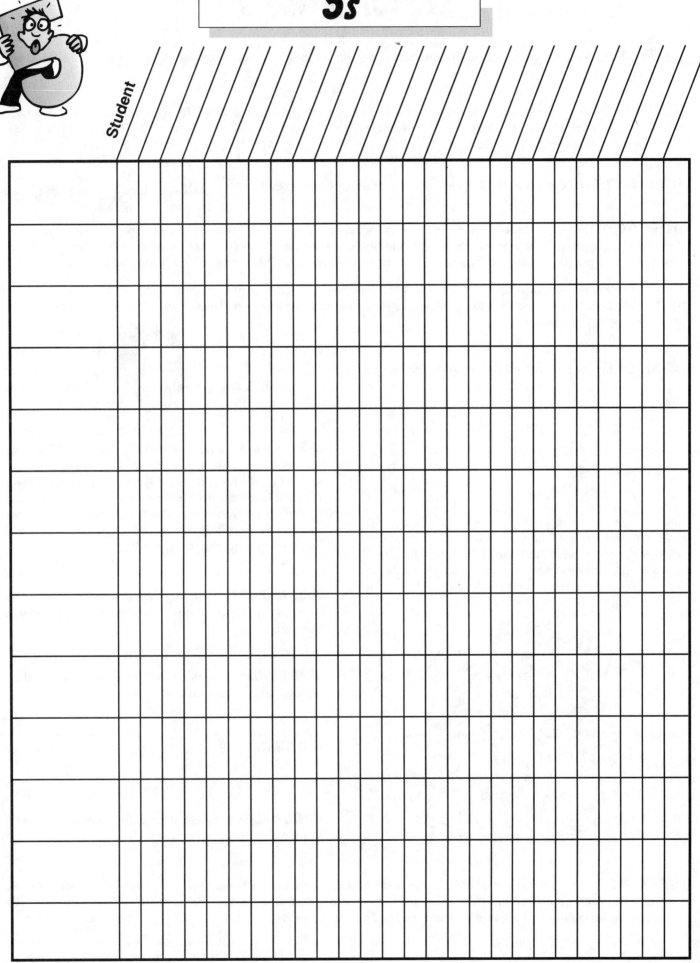

5s

Student

LESSON PLAN 8

OBJECTIVE: Mastering the 3s and 4s Groups. Students will learn these two key groups by means of routine drill, concrete manipulatives, charts and games.

MATERIALS: Practice Facts for 3s, 4s and 5s (page 62), Base 10 Counting Chart (page 24); Rectangular Arrays for 3s (page 65) and 4s (page 67); Travel Folders for 3s (page 68) and 4s (page 69); Worksheet for 3s, 4s and 5s (pages 70-71); Math Pack (page 66); Flash Cards for 3s and 4s (pages 29-38)

INTRODUCTION: Chant 10s, 11s, 12s and 5s. Chant other groups if necessary.

ATTENTION: Thorough knowledge of the 3s and 4s is the key to mastering the entire set of multiplication facts. Most of the previously taught groups have a simple rule to help students learn the facts. 3s, 4s, 6s, 7s and 8s are all difficult for students to remember. If 3s and 4s are mastered, only three facts remain to be learned. They are: 6 x 7, 6 x 8 and 7 x 8.

This can be demonstrated by crossing off all groups which have been previously taught including 3s and 4s; squares, 9s, 0s, 1s, 2s, 10s, 11s, 12s, 5s, 3s and 4s. Page 9 in this book illustrates this process of elimination. Demonstrate this to your students after they have mastered the 3s and 4s.

CHALLENGE: Find a repeating pattern in the answers to the 4s.
Answers:

4	8	12	16	20
24	28	32	36	40
44	48			

DO: Hand out or make Travel Folders for 3s and 4s. Students should master the first column so that they can count by 3s and 4s just as easily as by 5s or 10s. You could use a positive reinforcement such as a pizza certificate or candy bar for students who have mastered these two groups. Students need to know that these groups are very important.

DO: Teach 3s using the Base 10 Counting Chart as described in the section on 9s. Have students fill in the answers on the Rectangular Array for 3s. Pass out the Math Pack and have students cut out the cards for 3s. These can be studied and manipulated. Students should fill in the correct answers to the 3s on the Practice Facts for 3s, 4s and 5s. Repeat the above process for 4s.

ASSIGNMENT: Flash cards; Worksheet for 3s, 4s and 5s. Some of the materials in the "Do" section could be used as homework.

OPTIONAL: Fill in the 3s and 4s' answers on the blank Multiplication Facts Chart.

OPTIONAL: Worksheet G (page 72)—Web hexagons for extra drill on 3s, 4s and 5s.

OPTIONAL: Worksheet H (page 73)—More practice for 3s, 4s and 5s.

OPTIONAL: Use pipe cleaners and beads to help students with 3s and 4s. Use beads of different colors—red, white and blue, for example. For 3s, put three red, three white and three blue onto the pipe cleaner. Repeat until 12 sets of 3s have been arranged. Students can count the beads to learn the 3s. Do the same for 4s.

RECTANGULAR ARRAY FOR 3s

3 x 1 = _____

3 x 2 = _____

3 x 3 = _____

3 x 4 = _____

3 x 5 = _____

3 x 6 = _____

3 x 7 = _____

3 x 8 = _____

3 x 9 = _____

3 x 10 = _____

3 x 11 = _____

3 x 12 = _____

24	16	48
21	12	44
18	8	40
15	4	36
12	36	32
9	33	28
6	30	24
3	27	20

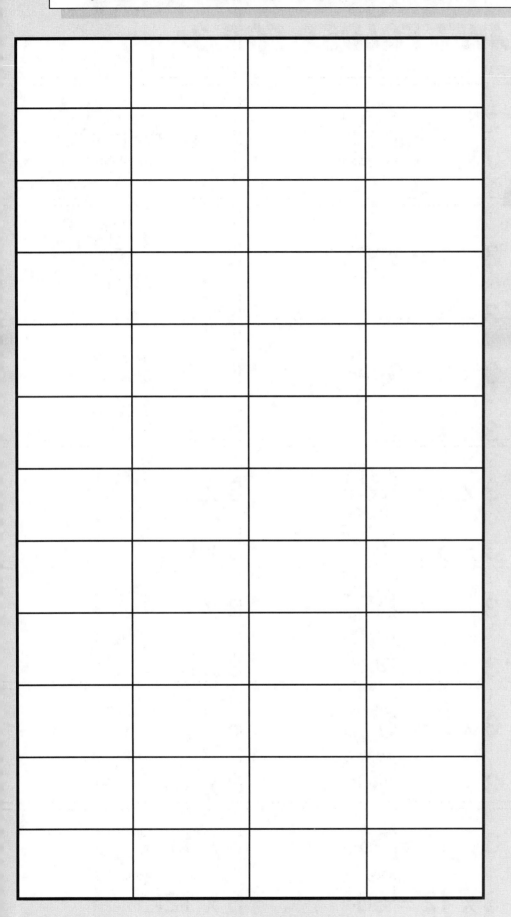

4 x 1 = ___

4 x 2 = ___

4 x 3 = ___

4 x 4 = ___

4 x 5 = ___

4 x 6 = ___

4 x 7 = ___

4 x 8 = ___

4 x 9 = ___

4 x 10 = ___

4 x 11 = ___

4 x 12 = ___

Name _____

3	3 x 1 = 3	3 x 1
6	3 x 2 = 6	3 x 2
9	3 x 3 = 9	3 x 3
12	3 x 4 = 12	3 x 4
15	3 x 5 = 15	3 x 5
18	3 x 6 = 18	3 x 6
21	3 x 7 = 21	3 x 7
24	3 x 8 = 24	3 x 8
27	3 x 9 = 27	3 x 9
30	3 x 10 = 30	3 x 10
33	3 x 11 = 33	3 x 11
36	3 x 12 = 36	3 x 12

Name _____

4	4 x 1 = 4	4 x 1
8	4 x 2 = 8	4 x 2
12	4 x 3 = 12	4 x 3
16	4 x 4 = 16	4 x 4
20	4 x 5 = 20	4 x 5
24	4 x 6 = 24	4 x 6
28	4 x 7 = 28	4 x 7
32	4 x 8 = 32	4 x 8
36	4 x 9 = 36	4 x 9
40	4 x 10 = 40	4 x 10
44	4 x 11 = 44	4 x 11
48	4 x 12 = 48	4 x 12

WORKSHEET FOR 3s, 4s AND 5s

1. **4 x 8** = ___

2. **3 x 3** = ___

3. **5 x 6** = ___

4. **3 x 10** = ___

5. **5 x 0** = ___

6. **3 x 0** = ___

7. **4 x 1** = ___

8. **4 x 2** = ___

9. **5 x 7** = ___

10. **4 x 9** = ___

11. **3 x 1** = ___

12. **5 x 1** = ___

13. **4 x 0** = ___

14. **3 x 2** = ___

15. **5 x 8** = ___

16. **3 x 8** = ___

17. **5 x 9** = ___

18. **4 x 4** = ___

19. **4 x 5** = ___

20. **5 x 2** = ___

Count by 3s: 3, 6, 9, ___, ___, ___, ___, ___, ___, ___, ___, ___

70

Name _____

21. **3 x 4 = ___**   33. **4 x 11 = ___**

22. **4 x 10 = ___**   34. **5 x 5 = ___**

23. **3 x 5 = ___**   35. **3 x 12 = ___**

24. **4 x 7 = ___**   36. **5 x 12 = ___**

25. **3 x 9 = ___**   37. **4 x 8 = ___**

26. **3 x 6 = ___**   38. **4 x 10 = ___**

27. **4 x 12 = ___**   39. **3 x 3 = ___**

28. **3 x 7 = ___**   40. **3 x 10 = ___**

29. **4 x 6 = ___**   41. **3 x 11 = ___**

30. **3 x 11 = ___**   42. **4 x 12 = ___**

31. **5 x 10 = ___**   43. **5 x 11 = ___**

32. **5 x 11 = ___**   44. **3 x 12 = ___**

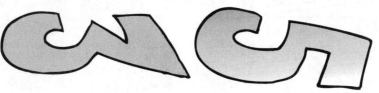

Count by 4s: 4, 8, 12, ___, ___, ___, ___, ___, ___, ___, ___, ___

Count by 5s: 5, 10, 15, ___, ___, ___, ___, ___, ___, ___, ___, ___

WEB WORK

Directions: Multiply the number in the center of the web by each number around it. Put each answer in the outer section of the web.

CHALLENGE: Can you make up a shortcut rule for multiplying a number by 1,000?

72

TLC10069 Copyright © Teaching & Learning Company, Carthage, IL 62321

Name _____

3s, 4s AND 5s

Directions: Write a multiplication problem to fit each story below. Find and label the answer.

1. David and his 2 friends have 7 baseball cards each. How many cards do the three friends have in all?

2. Robert collected 5 baseball cards each day for a week. How many cards did he collect for the week?

3. Jennifer earned 4 dollars a day baby-sitting at a neighbor's house. How much money did she earn for 8 days' work?

4. Colleen works with Jennifer, but she goes home sooner and only earns 3 dollars each day. How much does Colleen earn in 8 days?

5. Nick helps with repair work at the homeless shelter. He can pound 7 nails in 1 minute. How many nails can he pound in 5 minutes?

Directions: For each pair of multiplication facts, circle the answer which is larger. If the answers are the same, circle both.

6.	**3 x 5**	or	**4 x 4**	12.	**8 x 3**	or	**6 x 4**
7.	**3 x 2**	or	**4 x 1**	13.	**9 x 6**	or	**4 x 8**
8.	**4 x 9**	or	**5 x 7**	14.	**3 x 7**	or	**4 x 5**
9.	**3 x 6**	or	**5 x 4**	15.	**5 x 7**	or	**6 x 6**
10.	**4 x 7**	or	**5 x 5**	16.	**3 x 9**	or	**5 x 5**
11.	**3 x 8**	or	**5 x 5**	17.	**8 x 3**	or	**4 x 6**

18. Write all the multiplication facts we have studied which have an answer of 16, 18, 20 or 24. Use the Multiplication Facts Chart if necessary.

16	18	20	24

3s AND 4s

3 x 0																		
3 x 1																		
3 x 2																		
3 x 3																		
3 x 4																		
3 x 5																		
3 x 6																		
3 x 7																		
3 x 8																		
3 x 9																		
3 x 10																		
3 x 11																		
3 x 12																		
4 x 0																		
4 x 1																		
4 x 2																		
4 x 3																		
4 x 4																		
4 x 5																		
4 x 6																		
4 x 7																		
4 x 8																		
4 x 9																		
4 x 10																		
4 x 11																		
4 x 12																		

OBJECTIVE: Mastering the 6s, 7s and 8s Groups. Students will relate what they have already learned to these last three difficult groups. They will observe that only three facts remain to be learned. They will memorize the last three remaining facts—6 x 7, 6 x 8 and 7 x 8.

MATERIALS: Multiplication Facts Chart (page 77); Practice Facts for 6s, 7s and 8s (page 78); Worksheets for 6s, 7s and 8s (pages 79-80); Flash Cards for 6s, 7s and 8s (pages 29-38)

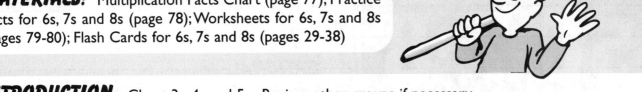

INTRODUCTION: Chant 3s, 4s and 5s. Review other groups if necessary.

Demonstrate to students that they know all but the last three facts: 6 x 7, 6 x 8 and 7 x 8

Use the wall-size Base 10 Counting Chart or overhead transparency and cross off all previously learned groups.

T-TABLES: Here is a classroom activity which can be used as a quiz, practice or timed test. This can be done at desks or on the board.

Students can draw their own T-tables, or a teacher can prepare a page of T-tables if preferred. Use this T format.

Students will write answers in the right-hand column.

After students have had some practice writing the answers in order, jumble the numbers in the left-hand column. This challenges the students to recall each answer individually.

Combine several T-tables for a quick quiz.

X	6
0	
1	
2	
3	
4	
5	
6	
7	
8	
9	
10	
11	
12	

If students are making their own T-tables, the teacher should dictate the jumbled numbers in the left-hand column so that all quizzes will be uniform.

For a classroom contest, divide the class into teams. Tally the correct answers for each team.

RULE: Teach the learning device for 7 x 8:
5, 6, 7, 8 or 56 = 7 x 8

HINT: For 6 x 7 and 6 x 8, recall that

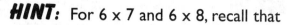

	$6 \times 6 = 36$
add another group of 6	$+6$
to get ...	$6 \times 7 = 42$
add another group of 6	$+6$
to get ...	$6 \times 8 = 48$

OPTIONAL: Fill in the last three answers on the blank Multiplication Facts Chart.

You could use the Base 10 Counting Chart and circle answers for these three groups, but I think it is better if students recall answers they have already learned for other groups to learn these last three groups.

ASSIGNMENT: Go through the Practice Facts for 6s, 7s and 8s with the students pointing out to them that they already know 6 x 0, 7 x 0 and 8 x 0 because they have learned the 0s. They already know all the 1s, 2s and so on.

Add the last three flash cards.

Chant facts in order for 6s, 7s and 8s.

After students have had a day or two to study, use the worksheets as an assignment.

OPTIONAL: Worksheet I (page 81)—Rectangular arrays of Xs for some of the 6s, 7s and 8s. Self-explanatory.

OPTIONAL: Worksheet J (page 82)—Additional practice. Self-explanatory.

MULTIPLICATION FACTS CHART

x	1	2	3	4	5	6	7	8	9	10	11	12
1	1	2	3	4	5	6	7	8	9	10	11	12
2	2	4	6	8	10	12	14	16	18	20	22	24
3	3	6	9	12	15	18	21	24	27	30	33	36
4	4	8	12	16	20	24	28	32	36	40	44	48
5	5	10	15	20	25	30	35	40	45	50	55	60
6	6	12	18	24	30	36	42	48	54	60	66	72
7	7	14	21	28	35	42	49	56	63	70	77	84
8	8	16	24	32	40	48	56	64	72	80	88	96
9	9	18	27	36	45	54	63	72	81	90	99	108
10	10	20	30	40	50	60	70	80	90	100	110	120
11	11	22	33	44	55	66	77	88	99	110	121	132
12	12	24	36	48	60	72	84	96	108	120	132	144

Name _____

6 x 0 = 0   7 x 0 = 0   8 x 0 = 0

6 x 1 = 6   7 x 1 = 7   8 x 1 = 8

6 x 2 = 12   7 x 2 = 14   8 x 2 = 16

6 x 3 = 18   7 x 3 = 21   8 x 3 = 24

6 x 4 = 24   7 x 4 = 28   8 x 4 = 32

6 x 5 = 30   7 x 5 = 35   8 x 5 = 40

6 x 6 = 36   7 x 6 = 42   8 x 6 = 48

6 x 7 = 42   7 x 7 = 49   8 x 7 = 56

6 x 8 = 48   7 x 8 = 56   8 x 8 = 64

6 x 9 = 54   7 x 9 = 63   8 x 9 = 72

6 x 10 = 60   7 x 10 = 70   8 x 10 = 80

6 x 11 = 66   7 x 11 = 77   8 x 11 = 88

6 x 12 = 72   7 x 12 = 84   8 x 12 = ___

Name _____

WORKSHEET FOR 6s, 7s AND 8s

1. **7 x 8** = ___
2. **6 x 3** = ___
3. **8 x 6** = ___
4. **6 x 10** = ___
5. **8 x 0** = ___
6. **6 x 0** = ___
7. **7 x 1** = ___
8. **7 x 2** = ___
9. **8 x 7** = ___
10. **7 x 9** = ___

11. **6 x 1** = ___
12. **8 x 1** = ___
13. **7 x 0** = ___
14. **6 x 2** = ___
15. **8 x 8** = ___
16. **6 x 8** = ___
17. **8 x 9** = ___
18. **7 x 4** = ___
19. **7 x 5** = ___
20. **8 x 2** = ___

Name _____

WORKSHEET FOR 6s, 7s AND 8s

21. **6 x 4** = ___

22. **7 x 10** = ___

23. **6 x 5** = ___

24. **7 x 7** = ___

25. **6 x 9** = ___

26. **6 x 6** = ___

27. **7 x 12** = ___

28. **6 x 7** = ___

29. **7 x 6** = ___

30. **6 x 11** = ___

31. **8 x 10** = ___

32. **8 x 11** = ___

33. **7 x 11** = ___

34. **8 x 5** = ___

35. **6 x 12** = ___

36. **8 x 12** = ___

37. **7 x 8** = ___

38. **7 x 10** = ___

39. **6 x 3** = ___

40. **6 x 10** = ___

41. **6 x 11** = ___

42. **7 x 12** = ___

43. **8 x 11** = ___

44. **6 x 12** = ___

Name _____

6s, 7s AND 8s

Directions: Make a rectangular array of Xs for each pair of numbers. Then count how many Xs are in each array.

Size of Array	Rectangular Array	How Many Xs?
6 x 3	x x x x x x x x x x x x x x x x x x	18
7 x 8		
6 x 8		
7 x 7		
6 x 7		
7 x 5		

CHALLENGE: The Blue Room has chairs in 7 rows with 6 chairs in each row. The Yellow Room has 6 rows of 8 chairs. The Green Room has 7 rows with 8 chairs in each. Which room will hold the Smith family reunion? Here are the families that will attend:

Samuel Smith: 2 adults, 4 children

Seymour Smith: 2 adults, 2 children

Samantha Smith: 1 adult, 2 children

Sarah Smith: 2 adults, 12 children

Sigmund Smith: 2 adults, 6 children

Sally Smith: 1 adult, 1 child

Sidney Smith: 1 adult, 3 children

Scott Smith: 3 adults, 4 children

Sissy Smith: 1 adult, 3 children

Frank Smith: 1 adult, 2 children

MULTIPLICATION FACTS CHART

Directions: Use a pencil to shade in each incorrect answer on this multiplication chart.

X	1	2	3	4	5	6	7	8	9	10	11	12
1	1	2	3	4	5	6	7	8	9	10	11	12
2	2	2	6	6	7	8	9	16	11	12	13	14
3	3	5	9	7	15	18	10	24	12	30	33	15
4	4	7	12	8	20	24	11	32	13	40	44	16
5	5	9	15	9	25	30	12	40	14	50	55	17
6	6	11	18	10	30	36	13	48	15	60	66	18
7	7	13	21	11	35	42	14	56	16	70	77	19
8	8	15	24	12	40	48	15	64	17	80	88	20
9	9	17	27	13	45	54	16	72	18	90	99	21
10	10	19	30	14	15	16	17	80	19	20	21	22
11	11	22	33	44	55	66	77	88	99	110	121	132
12	12	24	36	48	60	72	84	96	108	120	132	144

The shape of the shaded squares forms a number equal to $2^2 \times 5^2$. What is that number? _____

Student

6 x 0																				
6 x 1																				
6 x 2																				
6 x 3																				
6 x 4																				
6 x 5																				
6 x 6																				
6 x 7																				
6 x 8																				
6 x 9																				
6 x 10																				
6 x 11																				
6 x 12																				
7 x 0																				
7 x 1																				
7 x 2																				
7 x 3																				
7 x 4																				
7 x 5																				
7 x 6																				
7 x 7																				
7 x 8																				
7 x 9																				
7 x 10																				
7 x 11																				
7 x 12																				
8 x 0																				
8 x 1																				
8 x 2																				
8 x 3																				
8 x 4																				
8 x 5																				
8 x 6																				
8 x 7																				
8 x 8																				
8 x 9																				
8 x 10																				
8 x 11																				
8 x 12																				

OBJECTIVE: Students Will Review, Reinforce Their Knowledge and Be Rewarded. Students will be reviewing at all times throughout the *Math Phonics*™ units. They wll spend extra time reviewing through use of the assessment pages. They will be rewarded when they have learned all facts.

MATERIALS: Three Multiplication Assessment worksheets (pages 86-88), completed Multiplication Facts Chart (page 77), blank Multiplication Facts Chart (page 20), Math Phonics™ certificate (page 96), parents' Notes (pages 92 and 93), Flash Cards (pages 29-38)

INTRODUCTION: Have students bring in their Math Phonics Progess Chart and record their progress on the Teacher's Math Phonics Progress Chart. Chant 6s, 7s and 8s as a class. If necessary, give students a few days to study before giving the three pages of Multiplication Assessment worksheets.

DO: Give the Multiplication Assessment worksheets as a quiz in class. Give each student a complete copy of the Multiplication Facts Chart. Have them circle the ones missed on the Multiplication Assessment. Students should focus on learning the ones they missed. Have them write the ones they have missed 10 times each and take the assessment again.

Use a blank Multiplication Facts Chart as an in-class quiz.

Give a Math Phonics™ certificate to all students who have gotten all answers correct on the assessment.

Hold verbal (chanting) and written reviews (worksheets) periodically throughout the rest of the year. Use Note 4 to remind parents to work with their children.

CHALLENGE: Ask students to select one rule from the Summary of Rules (page 85) and design a poster illustrating the rule. Give each student a copy of the rules.

OPTIONAL: Worksheet K (page 89)–Additional practice. Self-explanatory.

OPTIONAL: Worksheet L (page 90)–Knowledge of prime numbers is very valuable in reducing fractions, finding common denominators and some types of algebra problems. This is a simple activity that can introduce students to the primes.

OPTIONAL: Worksheet M (page 91)–When students work long multiplication problems, they must first multiply and then add. Sometimes they add instead of multiplying or vice versa. This worksheet will help them become aware that they must pay attention to what they need to do. Send home parents' Note 4.

SUMMARY OF RULES

0s: Any number times 0 equals 0.

1s: Any number times 1 equals that same number.

2s: Any number times 2 is that number added to itself–the doubles in addition.

3s: Students learn to count by 3s. Use all Math Phonics™ materials for reinforcement.

4s: Students learn to count by 4s. Answers have a repeating pattern.

4	8	12	16	20
24	28	32	36	40
44	48			

5s: Five times an odd number ends in 5. Five times an even number ends in 0. For an even number, take half of the number you are multiplying by 5. Put that number in the 10s place of the answer.

6s: Sixes are learned with other groups except for 6 x 7 and 6 x 8. These are learned using Math Phonics™ materials to illustrate and reinforce.

7s: Sevens are learned with other groups except for 7 x 6 and 7 x 8. For 7 x 8, use this rule:

$$5, 6, 7, 8 \text{ or } 56 = 7 \times 8$$

8s: All are learned with other groups.

9s: Nines answers are in pairs. 18 and 81, 27 and 72, 36 and 63, 45 and 54. The number in the 10s place of the answer is one less than the number you are multiplying by 9. Numerals in one answer can be added together to equal 9. Use this rhyme:

> When multiplying 9, keep this mind:
> Look at a number in the answer line.
> Add the numerals together.
> They will equal 9.

10s: When multiplying a number by 10, add a 0 to the right of the number.

11s: When multiplying a number by 11, write that number in the 10s place and the 1s place of the answer.

12s: If you need to find a given number times 12, first find the answer for that number times 11. Add the first number to the 11s' answer.

SQUARES: Students calculate answers for themselves using the Perfect Squares activity sheet. Use Math Phonics™ materials for review and reinforcement.

Name _____

MULTIPLICATION ASSESSMENT

1. **12 x 2 =** ___

2. **3 x 1 =** ___

3. **11 x 3 =** ___

4. **6 x 9 =** ___

5. **8 x 7 =** ___

6. **2 x 5 =** ___

7. **0 x 2 =** ___

8. **10 x 6 =** ___

9. **8 x 8 =** ___

10. **4 x 6 =** ___

11. **9 x 9 =** ___

12. **4 x 2 =** ___

13. **7 x 9 =** ___

14. **9 x 8 =** ___

15. **10 x 10 =** ___

16. **11 x 7 =** ___

17. **12 x 3 =** ___

18. **0 x 0 =** ___

19. **5 x 6 =** ___

20. **7 x 7 =** ___

21. **3 x 4 =** ___

22. **1 x 6 =** ___

23. **5 x 3 =** ___

24. **7 x 4 =** ___

25. **12 x 6 =** ___

26. **10 x 11 =** ___

27. **3 x 3 =** ___

28. **3 x 0 =** ___

29. **9 x 5 =** ___

30. **4 x 8 =** ___

31. **0 x 1 =** ___

32. **2 x 2 =** ___

33. **7 x 5 =** ___

MULTIPLICATION ASSESSMENT

34. **10 x 4** = ___

35. **1 x 2** = ___

36. **4 x 0** = ___

37. **9 x 4** = ___

38. **10 x 7** = ___

39. **5 x 8** = ___

40. **1 x 1** = ___

41. **2 x 6** = ___

42. **11 x 8** = ___

43. **11 x 11** = ___

44. **2 x 3** = ___

45. **10 x 5** = ___

46. **11 x 6** = ___

47. **0 x 5** = ___

48. **6 x 3** = ___

49. **11 x 9** = ___

50. **1 x 4** = ___

51. **11 x 5** = ___

52. **12 x 8** = ___

53. **6 x 0** = ___

54. **10 x 9** = ___

55. **2 x 7** = ___

56. **12 x 12** = ___

57. **3 x 7** = ___

58. **12 x 7** = ___

59. **1 x 7** = ___

60. **12 x 5** = ___

61. **7 x 0** = ___

62. **8 x 2** = ___

63. **11 x 2** = ___

64. **0 x 8** = ___

65. **10 x 3** = ___

66. **9 x 1** = ___

Name _____

MULTIPLICATION ASSESSMENT

67. **2 x 9 =** ___

68. **6 x 8 =** ___

69. **10 x 8 =** ___

70. **10 x 12 =** ___

71. **1 x 8 =** ___

72. **9 x 0 =** ___

73. **10 x 2 =** ___

74. **11 x 4 =** ___

75. **7 x 6 =** ___

76. **5 x 4 =** ___

77. **10 x 1 =** ___

78. **3 x 8 =** ___

79. **12 x 0 =** ___

80. **10 x 0 =** ___

81. **4 x 4 =** ___

82. **11 x 1 =** ___

83. **5 x 1 =** ___

84. **11 x 0 =** ___

85. **9 x 3 =** ___

86. **5 x 5 =** ___

87. **12 x 9 =** ___

88. **6 x 6 =** ___

89. **11 x 12 =** ___

90. **12 x 1 =** ___

91. **12 x 4 =** ___

TLC10069 Copyright © Teaching & Learning Company, Carthage, IL 62321

Name _____

WHAT'S THE QUESTION?

WORKSHEET K

Directions: Here are some math answers. Below each number, write all the multiplication facts which would have that answer. The first three have been done for you. Some will have only one answer–that number times one. Use the Multiplication Facts Chart to help you.

15	16	17	18	19	20
1 x 15 = 15 3 x 5 = 15 5 x 3 = 15					

21	22	23	24	25	26

27	28	29	30	31	32

CHALLENGE: Jim's mother is 7 years more than 3 times his age. If Jim is 8, how old is his mother?

EXTRA CHALLENGE: I'm thinking of a number between 50 and 100. The answer is a perfect square. If you add the two numerals of the answer together, they equal 10. What is the number?

89

PRIMES

A prime is a number that is a multiple only of itself and 1. One is not considered a prime. Two is a prime and 3 is a prime. Four is not a prime because it is a multiple of 1, 2 and 4.

Find the primes in the Base 10 Counting Chart by following these steps:

1. Circle the 2 because it is a prime number. Cross out all numbers that are multiples of 2—all the even numbers.

2. Circle the 3 because it is a prime number. Cross out all numbers that are multiples of 3—that would be 6, 9, 12 and so on.

3. Four has already been crossed out because it is a multiple of 2. Circle 5 because it is a prime. Cross out all multiples of 5.

4. What is the next prime that you find on the chart? Circle that number. Cross out all multiples of that number. Most of those multiples have already been crossed off because that number times 2 was crossed off when we crossed off the multiples of 2. That number times 3 was crossed off with the multiples of 3.

5. What is the next prime that you find? Circle that number. Do we need to look at any multiples of that number? If so, cross them off.

6. Circle the next prime. Do we need to cross off multiples of that prime?

7. Continue until all primes have been circled up to 150, the end of the chart.

8. Write all the primes below.

2, 3, 5, _____, _____, _____, _____, _____, _____, _____, 31,

_____, _____, _____, _____, _____, _____, _____, _____, 71,

_____, _____, _____, _____, _____, 101, _____, _____, _____,

_____, 127, _____, _____, _____, 149

READ THE SIGNS!

Directions: Watch the signs on these problems.
Some are addition and some are multiplication.

1. 10 + 6	7. 8 + 0	13. 6 x 1	19. 8 + 9	25. 6 + 5	31. 11 x 6
2. 2 x 1	8. 6 x 0	14. 6 + 1	20. 7 x 4	26. 7 + 7	32. 10 x 8
3. 2 x 0	9. 7 + 1	15. 7 + 0	21. 7 + 5	27. 6 x 9	33. 11 + 8
4. 7 x 8	10. 7 x 2	16. 6 + 2	22. 8 x 2	28. 6 + 9	34. 8 x 5
5. 6 x 3	11. 8 + 7	17. 8 + 8	23. 6 x 4	29. 6 x 6	35. 8 + 5
6. 8 + 6	12. 7 x 9	18. 6 x 8	24. 10 + 7	30. 11 + 6	36. 7 x 8

I am interested in attending a Math Phonics™ training meeting.

Name: _____

Address: _____

Phone: _____

I am available at these times: _____

Dear Parents,

The Math Phonics™ training meeting will be held:

Date: _____

Time: _____

Place: _____

Please bring with you the pocket folder and all the Travel Folders, Practice Facts sheets and Worksheets which your child has brought home. The meeting will be over in 30 minutes, but you may stay a little longer if you have questions.

Sincerely,

DEAR PARENTS,

CONGRATULATIONS!

Your child mastered all 91 multiplication facts! This is a very important math skill, and I am happy that our class is doing so well at this time.

Please remember to review or drill every week or two. Going through the flash cards is an excellent way to review. Make two piles—one pile of the facts your child can say correctly and another of the ones he or she has missed. Continue to work on the "misses." If your child misses several in one group, get out that Travel Folder and review. Good luck!

Sincerely,

DEAR PARENTS,

We will start a review unit on multiplication tomorrow. Please practice the math facts tonight so the review will go well. Remember to use the Travel Folders, Practice Facts sheets, Math Pack, flash cards and games.

Sincerely,

Worksheet A, page 39

1. 9 x 3	7. Circle both	13. Bob
2. 9 x 9	8. Circle both	14. 399
3. 3 x 3	9. Circle both	15. 81
4. 9 x 1	10. 10 x 10	16. 63
5. 6 x 6	11. 11 x 11	17. 61
6. 7 x 7	12. 5 x 5	18. 144

Challenge: Answers will vary.

Worksheet B, page 40

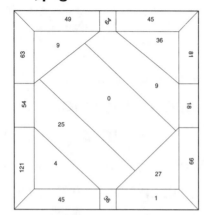

Worksheet C, page 50

1. 42	13. 35	25. 99
2. 63	14. 24	26. 80
3. 30	15. 66	27. 33
4. 44	16. 66	28. 80
5. 66	17. 33	29. 90
6. 22	18. 66	30. 45
7. 50	19. 60	31. 88
8. 36	20. 99	32. 44
9. 32	21. 16	33. 67
10. 26	22. 60	34. 68
11. 62	23. 90	35. 84
12. 48	24. 48	

Challenge: Answers will vary.

Worksheet D, page 51

Even x Even	Odd x Odd	Even x Odd
2 x 2 = 4	1 x 1 = 1	9 x 2 = 18
4 x 4 = 16	5 x 5 = 25	9 x 4 = 36
6 x 6 = 36	7 x 7 = 49	9 x 6 = 54
8 x 8 = 64	9 x 9 = 81	9 x 8 = 72
10 x 10 = 100	11 x 11 = 121	9 x 10 = 90
12 x 12 = 144	9 x 1 = 9	9 x 12 = 108
2 x 6 = 12	9 x 3 = 27	2 x 1 = 2
2 x 8 = 16	9 x 5 = 45	2 x 3 = 6
2 x 10 = 20	9 x 7 = 63	2 x 5 = 10
2 x 12 = 24	9 x 11 = 99	2 x 7 = 14
		2 x 11 = 2 2

1. even
2. odd
3. even

Challenge: 108 grams
Extra Challenge: 4 packs of hot dogs and 5 packs of buns

Worksheet E, page 57

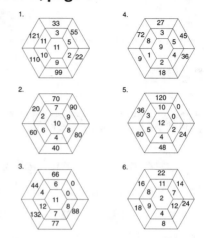

Worksheet F, page 58

1. 50	8. 800	15. 220	22. 230
2. 30	9. 100	16. 330	23. 108
3. 70	10. 110	17. 6500	24. Answers will vary.
4. 40	11. 120	18. 720	
5. 80	12. 200	19. 1320	
6. 400	13. 130	20. 2210	
7. 700	14. 150	21. 90	

Challenge: Answers will vary.
Extra Challenge: Answers will vary.

Worksheet G, page 72

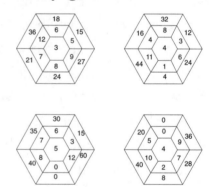

Worksheet H, page 73

1. 21	10. 4 x 7	18. 2 x 8 = 16
2. 35	11. 5 x 5	4 x 4 = 16
3. 32	12. Circle both	2 x 9 = 18
4. 24	13. 9 x 6	3 x 6 = 18
5. 35	14. 3 x 7	2 x 10 = 20
6. 4 x 4	15. 6 x 6	4 x 5 = 20
7. 3 x 2	16. 3 x 9	2 x 12 = 24
8. 4 x 9	17. Circle both	3 x 8 = 24
9. 5 x 4		4 x 6 = 24

Worksheet I, page 81

Size of Array	Rectangular of Array	How Many Xs?
6 x 3	XXXXXX XXXXXX XXXXXX	18
7 x 8	XXXXXXX XXXXXXX XXXXXXX XXXXXXX XXXXXXX	56
6 x 8	XXXXXX XXXXXX XXXXXX XXXXXX	48
7 x 7	XXXXXXX XXXXXXX XXXXXXX XXXXXXX	49
6 x 7	XXXXXX XXXXXX XXXXXX	42
7 x 5	XXXXXXX XXXXXXX XXXXXXX	35

Challenge: Green Room

Worksheet J, page 82

Directions: Use a pencil to shade in each incorrect answer on this multiplication chart.

X	1	2	3	4	5	6	7	8	9	10	11	12
1	1	2	3	4	5	6	7	8	9	10	11	12
2	2	2	6	6	7	8	9	16	11	12	13	14
3	3	5	9	7	15	18	10	24	12	30	33	15
4	4	7	12	8	20	24	11	32	13	40	44	16
5	5	9	15	9	25	30	12	40	14	50	55	17
6	6	11	18	10	30	36	13	48	15	60	66	18
7	7	13	21	11	35	42	14	56	16	70	77	19
8	8	15	24	12	40	48	15	64	17	80	88	20
9	9	17	27	13	45	54	16	72	18	90	99	21
10	10	19	30	14	15	16	17	80	19	20	21	22
11	11	22	33	44	55	66	77	88	99	110	121	132
12	12	24	36	48	60	72	84	96	108	120	132	144

The shape of the shaded squares forms a number equal to $2^2 \times 5^2$. What is that number? __100__

Worksheet K, page 89

15	16	17	18	19	20
1 x 15 = 15 3 x 5 = 15 5 x 3 = 15	1 x 16 = 16 2 x 8 = 16 4 x 4 = 16	1 x 17 = 17	1 x 18 = 18 2 x 9 = 18 3 x 6 = 18	1 x 19 = 19	1 x 20 = 20 2 x 10 = 20 4 x 5 = 20

21	22	23	24	25	26
1 x 21 = 21 3 x 7 = 21	1 x 22 = 22 2 x 11 = 22	1 x 23 = 23	1 x 24 = 24 2 x 12 = 24 3 x 8 = 24 4 x 6 = 24	1 x 25 = 25 5 x 5 = 25	1 x 26 = 26 2 x 13 = 26

27	28	29	30	31	32
1 x 27 = 27 3 x 9 = 27	1 x 28 = 28 2 x 14 = 28 4 x 7 = 28	1 x 29 = 29	1 x 30 = 30 2 x 15 = 30 3 x 10 = 30 5 x 6 = 30	1 x 31 = 31	1 x 32 = 32 2 x 16 = 32 4 x 8 = 32

Challenge: 31
Extra Challenge: 64

Worksheet L, page 90

4. 7
5. 11, yes
6. 13, no
8. 2, 3, 5, 7, 11, 13, 17, 19,
   23, 29, 31, 37, 41, 43, 47,
   53, 59, 61, 67, 71, 73, 79,
   83, 89, 97, 101, 103, 107,
   109, 113, 127, 131, 137,
   139, 149

Worksheet M, page 91

1. 16	13. 6	25. 11
2. 2	14. 7	26. 14
3. 0	15. 7	27. 54
4. 56	16. 8	28. 15
5. 18	17. 16	29. 36
6. 14	18. 48	30. 17
7. 8	19. 17	31. 66
8. 0	20. 28	32. 80
9. 8	21. 12	33. 19
10. 14	22. 16	34. 40
11. 15	23. 24	35. 13
12. 63	24. 17	36. 56

CONGRATULATIONS!

_____

**knows the
multiplication facts 0-12.**

_____
signed

_____
date

CONGRATULATIONS!

YOU ARE A

MULTIPLICATION

MASTER!

_____
signed

_____
date